THE TASTE OF OUR TIME

Collection planned and directed by

ALBERT SKIRA

BIOGRAPHICAL AND CRITICAL STUDY
BY
EUGENIO BATTISTI

Translated from the Italian by James Emmons

GIOTTO

SKIRA

Title page:
Scenes from the Life of Joachim: The Annunciation to St Anne
(detail), 1305-1306. Fresco. Scrovegni Chapel, Padua.

✳

© by Editions d'Art Albert Skira, 1960.
Library of Congress Catalog Card Number: 60-8730.

✳

Distributed in the United States by
THE WORLD PUBLISHING COMPANY
2231 West 110th Street - Cleveland 2, Ohio

GIOTTO studies have reached a decisive turning point. A careful sifting of the available documents is now making it possible to establish a more satisfactory chronology of the artist's œuvre. Recent restorations of the Santa Croce frescos in Florence have yielded almost miraculous results. Cleared of 19th-century repainting, the frescos in the Bardi Chapel have revealed an unexpected freedom of handling and coloristic verve; those in the Peruzzi Chapel have confirmed the unprecedented monumentality so much admired in the High Renaissance. Many panel paintings too, by Giotto or his school, have been restored to something very like their original state. In the same way, with the work of cleaning now in progress, visitors to the Scrovegni Chapel in Padua will soon be able to appreciate unsuspected refinements of color in the frescos there.

We find ourselves, then, nearly seven hundred years after Giotto's birth, in the presence of a group of really admirable works, easily accessible, which modern techniques of reproduction enable us to compare in their minutest details, and which every tourist to Italy makes a point of seeing. Never has Giotto's fame been so great as it is now. Innumerable studies and monographs have been devoted to him, while technical analyses of his great fresco cycles have reached the stage where we can almost follow their development day by day, can almost fathom the master mind behind them, and even grasp the mainsprings of his craftsmanship as well as his artistry, the human side of the man as well as his genius.

Yet, for all this, Giotto remains profoundly enigmatic. Equally enigmatic remain the origins of monumental painting in Tuscany. The problems so far solved have given rise to a thousand others, which call for solution in turn. In the light of the authentic documents, not only the older interpretations of Giotto but even the most recent seem biased or out of date.

Our analytical method also contains an element of uncertainty. If we confine our study to autograph works, in which the artist's hand seems to have left its mark, then Giotto's world, already grievously diminished by so many losses, appears narrow indeed in view of the fame it enjoys and the impact it has had. If on the other hand we enlarge the field of scrutiny, we do so at the risk of losing any valid criterion of judgment. His pupils and imitators, the Trecento critics and his Renaissance admirers, all contributed to create what might be called the Giotto myth. And the historical importance of this myth is in a sense greater than that of Giotto himself. Like Cubism in our time, Giottism grew into a movement transcending any single personality, evolving in accordance with laws of its own.

This is true, however, not only of the greatest of Trecento painters, but of many masters of Italian art. One of the foremost architects, thinkers and men of taste of Renaissance times, Leon Battista Alberti, who in some ways resembled Giotto, remains something of a riddle as far as his own individuality goes, in spite of the thorough knowledge we have of his masterpieces. This is largely due to the fact that these great personalities left the execution of much of their work to pupils and assistants, or better, created, in addition to their own personal style, a collective style; they became the moving spirit of a whole society, and besides being artists were men of action. So that to confine ourselves to their autograph works amounts, in effect, to removing them bodily from a much larger historical and cultural context. But on the other hand, if we fail to go back from the myth to the individual, then we shall also fail to trace to their source those currents of influence which, owing both to personal merit and to the fortunate circumstance that the time was ripe for them, became the collective language of several generations of artists.

The aim of this brief study, needless to say, is not to solve these or other problems. As against the Giotto we take for granted today, however, it is hoped that from these pages will emerge a picture of Giotto as he must have been seen and judged by his contemporaries. As we examine the problems he had to cope with, particularly those of subject and content, we must remember that Giotto was after all a painter of religious and historical subjects rather than a pure artist; he was alive to the great religious, political and social issues of his time, and his attitude toward them, whether he was for or against, is clearly and consciously reflected in his style.

THE LAST JUDGMENT, DETAIL: ANGEL UNFURLING THE HEAVENS, 1304.
FRESCO, SCROVEGNI CHAPEL, PADUA.

BIOGRAPHICAL RECORDS

WE have far more records and testimonies relating to Giotto than to any other earlier or contemporary artist. With him moreover begins art criticism, which at first, in imitation of the ancients, was mainly biographical. Giotto, in other words, was acknowledged to be as deserving of applause and commemoration as a great *condottiere* or a famous man of letters. The figurative arts, hitherto dismissed as mere handicrafts, became a humanist discipline thanks to him.

We find him described as a man of culture and learning, avid of glory. His works were recorded in town chronicles; such was the case at both Padua and Florence. He was spoken of with reverence by famous writers like Petrarch, Boccaccio and Francesco da Barberino. Dante mentions him. In Florence he was a national hero. The *novella* writers seized on him as a character well suited to enliven their tales, and put jokes and witticisms into his mouth; the picture they give is that of a shrewd and sturdy burgher, with a ready wit, at times of a rude and popular cast. Legends sprang up around his name, picturing him as a precocious genius, early surpassing his teacher, almost at once a recognized master. Even when we make allowance for some ingenuousness and the frequent use of stock phrases often derived from classical authors, the Trecento and Quattrocento documents that we have all agree in one particular: the extraordinary novelty of Giotto's style and the force of his personality. In time this impression crystallized in an outright assertion, to the effect that with Giotto the dead art of painting was resurrected and given a new lease of life. The most solemn expression of this idea is perhaps that given in 1440 by Aeneas Silvius Piccolomini (the future Pius II), who, much as Giotto's immediate contemporaries had done, associated the new flowering of painting and the arts with the renewal of letters and culture in general. "As literature fell into decay, so painting too declined. When the former recovered, the latter also lifted up its head. We have seen that for two hundred years painting had none of the refinements of art. The writings of that period are rude, inept, uncouth. After Petrarch letters revived. After Giotto the painter's hand regained its powers, and we have already seen both letters and painting attain the summit of art" (*Epistulae*, CXIX, Lugano 1518).

So Giotto, together with Petrarch, came to be regarded as the very founder of the Renaissance—an interpretation which, while certainly straining the facts of history, indicates the importance of his cultural even more than his artistic legacy. As for the masters who came after him, not only Masaccio and Donatello pored over his work, but so did Michelangelo, who extolled its expressive power. We today are more inclined to see the Trecento side of Giotto's art. And this shift of emphasis predisposes us to accuse the early critics of partiality, for by making an abstract idol of the real man, they quite ignored some of his most peculiar characteristics and fostered a confusion of attributions that increased with time. But our position, after all, is no doubt as biased as theirs.

Giotto's fame in his lifetime was also unusual in another respect, as even Dante seems to imply: he became a fashionable artist. Popes and princes vied for his services, at Padua, Naples, Milan, Rome. Already in his early works in Rome he conveys the impression of being a typical court painter. He owed his fame indeed to his outstanding abilities, but also to the fact that his taste coincided with the modern-minded, classicizing tendencies of the humanists of his day. As one of his distant followers, Cennino Cennini, said of him, "he translated the art of painting from Greek into Latin." With Giotto, then, Italy first acquired a truly national art, one which, moreover (though this view is historically indefensible), was regarded as a direct and spontaneous rebirth of antiquity: hence more universal, more legitimate than the Byzantine tradition. Giotto was thus credited with renewing the link with past glories that had been too long eclipsed, and with gathering in their heritage. What the *signorie*, as heirs of Rome, and above all the pope were trying to do politically, Giotto did far more successfully in art. He was accordingly regarded, down to the end of the 19th century and even beyond, as one of the great champions of Italian nationhood, and, together with Dante, as the supreme national hero. Art, for once, overshadowed politics.

Set forth below, with a few comments, are the known facts of Giotto's life:

1266. Probable date of his birth at Colle di Vespignano in the valley of the Mugello, a few miles north of Florence. His father, Bondone, who had already moved to Florence some years before, was a native of this locality, with which Giotto himself remained closely connected, later acquiring houses and land there. At Colle, or in the neighborhood, his wife, his sons (one of whom became prior of the church of San Martino) and three of his daughters came to live. The name Giotto is a diminutive, presumably of Angiolo, the name of his paternal grandfather.

After 1272. Enters the workshop of Cimabue in Florence, after this painter's return from Rome. It is not known for certain which of his master's works in Florence or elsewhere Giotto may have had a share in while still an apprentice.

About 1290. Paints for his parish church, Santa Maria Novella, in Florence, the large crucifix which now hangs in the sacristy. Marries Monna Cinta di Lapo del Pela, who bore him several sons and daughters.

1296-1297 (?). Commissioned by Fra Giovanni di Murro, new minister general of the Franciscans, to paint the fresco cycle devoted to St Francis in the Upper Church of San Francesco at Assisi. This work shows a certain familiarity with Roman culture and makes it likely that he had already been to Rome.

1298. Executes the mosaic known as the "Navicella," in the atrium of Old St Peter's in Rome, commissioned by Cardinal Jacopo Stefaneschi.

1300. Paints a fresco commemorating the proclamation of the Jubilee of 1300 by Pope Boniface VIII, in the loggia of the Lateran Basilica.

1301. Mentioned as being the owner of a house in Florence, near Santa Maria Novella. Presumably he had left Rome by now. The frescos and polyptych (now in the Uffizi) which he painted for the new Badia in Florence may date from this time.

From 1303 (?). Continues to work for the Franciscans, painting frescos (now lost) of the miracles of St Anthony of Padua in their church at Rimini, known today as the Tempio Malatestiano, and decorating the tomb of the same saint in the basilica of Sant'Antonio at Padua.

1304-1306. Frescos in the Scrovegni Chapel at Padua. He was certainly absent from Florence in 1305, as he is known to have leased his house for that year.

From 1307. Paintings on astrological themes in the great hall of the Palazzo della Ragione in Padua, on subjects supplied by the famous astrologer and physician Pietro d'Abano (now lost or repainted).

From 1311. Giotto seems now to have made his home in Florence, where his name occurs in different records as standing surety for a loan (which shows that he must have been fairly well off). Hires out a loom at a very high rate of payment. Buys and sells land in the Mugello. He becomes in time a wealthy landowner.

1313. Gives the power of attorney to a certain Benedetto, son of the late Pace, in order to recover some household articles he had left in Rome; which seems to indicate either that he intended to make a trip to Rome or, more probably, in view of the tragic economic plight of the city after the pope's removal to Avignon, that he had decided to discontinue whatever *pied-à-terre* he may have kept there.

After 1317. Paints, among many other works cited in early records, scenes from the life of St Francis in the Bardi Chapel in Santa Croce, Florence. Four chapels in this Franciscan church are mentioned as being frescoed by Giotto; only two of these decorations have survived. Also lost is the fresco representing the "Comune Rubato" in the Palazzo del Podestà (Bargello); this was one of the most important allegorical paintings of the period.

1327. Enrols along with Taddeo Gaddi, Bernardo Daddi and other painters in the guild of physicians and apothecaries, to which artists were only admitted from this date on.

1329-1333. Works in Naples at the court of Robert of Anjou, whose intimate friend and familiar he becomes. Among other things, he paints a series of famous men in the Castelnuovo, and decorates the palace chapel and the Castel dell'Uovo. None of these works has survived.

After 1330-before 1334. May have gone to Bologna to paint the altarpiece now in the Pinacoteca and to decorate a chapel in the Castello di Galliera.

1334. On April 12 he is appointed master of the works of the cathedral of Florence, succeeding Arnolfo di Cambio, and official architect of the city walls and fortifications. The foundation stone of the Campanile is laid on July 19, and the lower courses are built under Giotto's personal supervision.

1335-1336. Summoned to Milan by Azzone Visconti to execute a "Vana Gloria" with, around it, the "most illustrious ancient princes of the world," and perhaps some frescos in the palace church of San Gottardo (all lost).

1337 (January 8). After his return to Florence, dies at the age of seventy and is interred in the church of Santa Croce, in a humble tomb marked only by a plain marble plaque.

Of Giotto's family the few recorded facts we have are as follows. His father, Bondone, was still alive in 1305. A certain Martino, a blacksmith, may have been the painter's brother. Of Giotto's daughters three married in the Val di Mugello; another joined a religious sisterhood attached to Santa Maria Novella in Florence and died shortly after her father. One son, Francesco, who came of age in 1318, became prior of the church of San Martino at Colle; he looked after his father's affairs.

According to Ghiberti, his outstanding pupils were Stefano, Taddeo Gaddi, and Maso. But Giotto's direct influence extended to a much wider circle of artists. Wherever he worked he founded a local school of painting, very fine schools in many cases, which proved capable of developing characteristics of their own and sustaining them throughout the century.

GIOTTO AND HIS TIMES

GIOTTO AND SCULPTURE

To form a clear and equitable judgment of Giotto's work, we must begin by rectifying several misconceptions, due in part to the chauvinism of his Tuscan biographers, such as Vasari, and in part to insufficient knowledge of the historical realities of the age in which the great painter lived and worked. The most serious fallacy concerns the "absolute originality" of Giotto's style. Well known are the famous epitaph composed by Angelo Poliziano at the behest of Lorenzo di Medici (beginning *"Ille ego sum, per quam pictura extinta revixit..."*) and the tribute of praise paid him shortly after his death by Boccaccio, according to whom Giotto "restored to the light that art which, for many centuries, through the mistaken ways of those who painted rather to charm the eyes of the ignorant than to gratify the intelligence of the wise, had lain in its grave."

Now the 13th century was rich in masterpieces. Very close in time to Giotto come the extraordinary achievements in sculpture of Nicola and Giovanni Pisano, and the masterpieces, equally fine, of the anonymous sculptors of Northern Europe, at Reims, Bamberg, Bourges and Naumburg, for example. Let us remember too the very close relations, often amounting to dependency on Giotto's part, between him and Arnolfo di Cambio. Giotto, it is true, rediscovered the plastic values of painting, gave an object lesson in concrete figurative power which thereafter remained fundamental for the whole of Italian art, and solved the problem of pictorial representation in a way that was altogether new. His scenes are not sketchy or allusive, but solid, tangible, tightly constructed, rigorous not only in the delineation, but in the expression and attitudes. But he could never have attained these qualities without the lessons sculpture taught him. As a painter, Giotto must have realized that his art had lagged behind that of the sculptors by nearly seventy years. He therefore joined the classicizing movement, almost certainly connected with the renewed patronage of the arts, which got under way about the third decade of the 13th century, and which in Italy coincided with the fabulous activities of Frederick II. With new times had come a new art, answering to a more modern conception of life, for which Byzantine painting and its dramatic expressionism could no longer provide an adequate language. So it was mainly in sculpture and architecture that the decisive transition was accomplished, all over Europe, from so-called medieval symbolism to what is usually styled Gothic naturalism, which in fact became the basis of all modern Western art up to Impressionism.

So-called Gothic naturalism had already reached maturity by the time Giotto appeared. Yet—and herein lies his greatness—he availed himself of the new style to express, in painting, a much wider range of themes and moods than any sculptor had done. Renaissance writers dwell on the universality of painting, on the painter's ability to capture and record every aspect of reality in his own idiom, while the limits of sculpture are admittedly narrower and its subject matter less varied. Painting very probably owes this universality largely to Giotto. From sculpture he took no more than the notion and the canons of plasticism, exercising great freedom as regards iconography and subject matter; he seldom based his work on specific ancient models, and even as compared with such great artists as Arnolfo di Cambio and Giovanni Pisano, he was much freer, much more imaginative. Rich with this plastic and pictorial experience, he attempted to reproduce every aspect of the external world, with results that in many cases set the standard for coming generations; but in doing so he consistently reshaped the trend toward naturalism, guiding it away from the accidental back to the exemplary. Boccaccio very rightly said of him: "He had so excellent a skill, that there was nothing in nature, mother of all things and agent of the ceaseless circling of the heavens, which he with stylus and pen and brush did not depict so very like to what it appeared, that many a time with his handiwork it came about that the eyes of men were led into error, taking for real what was only painted."

Already at Assisi fine details can be singled out which show how keen an observer Giotto was of flowers, trees, animals, landscapes, architecture, perspective effects, light and shade, human types and costume, all recorded with unparalleled lifelikeness. In his hands, notwithstanding the severely geometrical, idealizing structure of every scene, the stock repertory of symbols used by untold generations of artists for sacred episodes was straightway renewed. From now on the heroes of biblical and sacred history appeared on a real stage (anticipating the scenography of sacred plays), and a stage so well defined spatially as to locate the action in a fully developed architectonic and atmospheric setting. The result was impressive: the sacred scene, unexpectedly removed from the supernatural plane, was brought to earth, brought into the home, into daily life, almost as if to show that the gap between the sacred and profane was very slight. And if the sphere of the sacred appeared to shrink alarmingly from what it had been in the mystical vision of the Middle Ages, the sphere of the profane came to assume a dignity and gravity it had never known in any other period or civilization. When the Florentine humanists later described man as an earthly god, they may well have had the memory of Giotto's wonderful, untiring activity in mind, and his monumental figures in their mind's eye.

This new sense of reality is usually associated with Franciscan thought, and rightly so—but only within certain limits.

That Giotto was sincerely devoted to St Francis is proved by his christening one of his sons Francesco and one of his daughters Chiara; by the fact that much of his work, and much of the work of his school, was done at Assisi; and by the many commissions he received for paintings in Franciscan churches, at Rimini, Padua, Florence. Franciscan iconography was boldly renewed by Giotto and his followers. All this is indisputable.

Giotto, however, was not the painter of the rightful followers of St Francis, i.e. of the *poverelli*, the Zealots or Spirituals who regarded Rome as a sink of iniquity. Indeed, had the testament of the founder been observed, had the order maintained the original ideal of poverty, then very probably Giotto would never have been asked to decorate a Franciscan church. As late as 1279 the general chapter laid down the following policy: "Forasmuch as curious and unnecessary ornaments contravene the vow of poverty, we decree that the decoration of sacred edifices, in pictures, carvings, windows, columns and the like, should be strictly avoided." Frescos, sculpture and stained glass, then, were to be excluded from the churches of the order, as out of keeping with those principles of austerity which have been consistently observed to the present day by the Cistercians. It was only by violating the decrees of 1279 that the church of Assisi was able to become not only the most highly decorated basilica in Europe, but for a period of over fifty years probably the most fervent center of religious painting that Italy has ever known. And this flagrant breach of the Franciscan Rule must have aroused a wave of indignation, to judge by the long resistance of the Zealots of the order, outside Italy in particular, to every attempt at church decoration.

This is confirmed, furthermore, by the early iconography of Franciscan art. The life and miracles of St Francis illustrated, for example, in the panel of 1235 at Pescia are, for all their dramatic intensity, treated in a deliberately hieratic and symbolic spirit; and the attempt to heighten the emotional power of the scenes leads to schematizations and cadences which recall the rhythm of a Gregorian chant. The narrative unfolds, in other words, on lines which do not pretend to be lifelike and objective, but which lay emphasis on specific motifs, usually symbolic, at the expense of others; on, for example, the intentness with which the birds—perhaps an allusion to those of the Apocalypse—listen to the preaching of the saint; on the bleak and lonely landscape around the hermitage to which, like a biblical prophet, he loved to withdraw. Even in the face of the saint, who after all was a well-known contemporary, we find little concern on the artist's part to produce a recognizable likeness, but rather a dramatic insistence on his asceticism and saintliness.

Apart from the legend of the *poverello*, the only theme treated by the early Franciscan iconography, in common as a matter of fact with other orders, was that of the suffering Christ, with the Virgin and St John at His side; a theme of the utmost pathos, perhaps of Benedictine origin, rendered with an almost paroxysmal linearism and expressionism. All this, moreover, is quite in keeping with the apocalyptic, messianic spirit of early Franciscanism. Today, with the famous poem of the "Praises of the Creatures" uppermost in our minds, we tend, in spite of ourselves, to view it in a romantic, or anyhow a Petrarchian, light. But undoubtedly the saint's invocations to all the creatures and elements of the earth are predominantly, if not exclusively, cosmological in meaning; and the structure of this same poem is wholly ritualistic.

In addition to this indirect evidence, we have a further token of Giotto's attitude, and one of considerable interest. This is a ballad against poverty, already attributed to him at a very early date; so that, even if not his own, it may be taken as being in substantial agreement with what were known to be his ideas. Poverty, to which the "party of relaxation" within the Franciscan order itself strenuously objected, was accused by Giotto of "extinguishing the good," of sullying the honor of ladies and maidens, of conducing to theft, violence and outrage. Those who advocate it are dismissed as hypocrites and rogues; the condition of poverty is not only unnatural to man, but corrupting, for as his song puts it, *"rade volte estremo è senza vizio"* (an extreme is seldom without vice). He goes on to compare a society founded on poverty to an edifice without foundations, and therefore unable to withstand wind and weather. The whole tone of the ballad is harsh and haughty; its arguments strike home. They proceed from a truly humanistic spirit, one that makes its appeal not only to the ethics of antiquity, for virtue, it seems to say, is not a mystical yearning but a logical norm, a middle way between two extremes; in this instance between avarice and poverty; between, socially speaking, an oligarchy of the wealthy and an absence of civil organization. It is certainly no accident that, in the allegorical series of Virtues in the Scrovegni Chapel at Padua, the only one to wear a crown, as queen of all the others, is Justice; for she does not repudiate earthly possessions but distributes them equally and stimulates social activities.

Obviously we are not to interpret this attitude as a form of selfishness, even if Giotto was a shrewd administrator of his property (he hired out looms at a high rental to workmen who were too poor to buy their own). What it does seem to reflect is a strong preference for the active as against the contemplative life, and in Giotto no misgivings, no moral doubts, are to be discerned. His confident optimism in the potential achievements of man—it is not for nothing that he was the first to paint picture cycles glorifying ancient heroes—went considerably beyond that partial revaluation of man and the world proposed by St Bonaventura even more explicitly than by St Bernard. For this Ulysses of painting the known world had ceased to be bounded by the pillars of Hercules.

GIOTTO AND DANTE

Since Dante too is held up as a champion of humanity, it was inevitable that he should be compared with Giotto, the more so as both were Florentines. The tradition of their friendship moreover, and even of a collaboration between them in devising the frescos in the Scrovegni Chapel, is a very old one. It rests on the famous comparison of Giotto with Cimabue in Canto XI of the Purgatorio:

> *Credette Cimabue nella pittura*
> *Tener lo campo, e ora ha Giotto il grido,*
> *Si che la fama di colui è oscura*

> (Cimabue thought to hold the field
> In painting, and now Giotto hath the cry,
> So that the fame of Cimabue is obscured),

and on the anecdote handed down by Benvenuto da Imola of a meeting at Padua between the painter, then a young man, and the poet. Then there is the fact that a few years after Giotto's death, his pupils included a portrait of Dante in some frescos they painted in the chapel of the Palazzo del Podestà in Florence. So the tradition seems to be well founded, and has accordingly led several times to comparisons between Giotto's frescos and the Divine Comedy, both from the iconographical point of view (with the disappointing conclusion that there is practically no connection between them) and from the stylistic point of view, in an effort to trace some affinity of taste between them.

Now while there can be no doubt that both Giotto and Dante consciously belonged to a new age, had a very similar grasp of reality, a similar rational-minded temper and outlook, a similar power of vivid representation, and lived in the same heroic climate, even where their religious convictions were concerned, the fact remains that, when all is said and done, the two men form a sharp and well-nigh irreconcilable contrast; a contrast that may readily be construed, assuming they actually met, as a party conflict.

That Giotto had ties with the theocratic party of Rome, or anyhow was favorably regarded by the higher echelons of the ecclesiastical hierarchy, is shown by the number and importance of the official commissions he received both in Rome and from the Conventual Franciscans, the monastic order most closely attached to the Roman pontificate at that time. Now Dante's hostility toward Pope Boniface VIII, protector of the Conventuals, is notorious, and this divergence could hardly have failed to affect the relations between the two great men. Signs of some such conflict can be detected in the Divine Comedy. The lines referring to Giotto are usually quoted out of their context, and so interpreted as a eulogy. But if we take the trouble to read the whole canto (which deals with the proud and arrogant), we realize that this so-called eulogy is far less complimentary than is commonly supposed. Dante by no means exalts the fame of the artists to whom he alludes, but laments the "empty glory of human powers," and the brevity of it, doomed to eclipse as new fashions succeed the old.

> Non è il mondan romore altro ch'un fiato
> Di vento, ch'or vien quinci e or vien quindi,
> E muta nome perchè muta lato.

> (Earthly fame is naught but a breath
> Of wind, which now cometh hence and now thence,
> And changeth name as it changeth direction.)

The only inference to be drawn from the famous passage in Canto XI is that, when Dante was composing the Purgatorio, Giotto's fame was already great; his name, presumably, was on everyone's lips. But Dante, as if deliberately taking the opposite view, publicly warned him against the sin of pride, citing him among the candidates for Purgatory, and insinuating that he in turn will be followed by others, who will behave toward him as he has behaved toward Cimabue. This, as it so happened, was never the case; the prophecy implied in Dante's lines was never fulfilled. These lines, then, though instrumental in securing Giotto's later fame, were not intended as a tribute of praise. Cimabue in fact was already dead when they were written; and, as Vasari suggested, the words *"Credette Cimabue nella pittura tener lo campo"* may be no more than a translation into the vernacular of the master's epitaph: *"Credidit ut Cimabos picturae castra tenere..."*

Even apart from this innuendo, which posterity misconstrued as praise, Dante, in keeping with his principles, showed himself bitterly hostile to the friends and patrons of Giotto. To Pope Boniface VIII first of all, to whom Giotto probably owed his reputation in the first instance, on the strength of the great works, commissioned by Boniface, on public view in the Lateran basilica and St Peter's. According to Dante, the apostle's tomb had been turned into a sewer, not only because the popes were guilty of simony but—as we infer from an allusion to the charges made against Boniface VIII by Philip the Fair of France —because they had revived idolatrous practices.

> *Fatto v'avete Dio d'oro e d'argento*
> *Che altro è da voi all'idolatre.*

> (You have made you a god of gold and silver,
> And wherein do you differ from the idolater?)

> (Inferno, Canto XIX).

In connection with the Franciscans, Dante alludes again and again to the fundamental importance of poverty, thus siding with the party opposed to Giotto. For Dante, Poverty reigns supreme among the virtues and deserves to be crowned; we find in the Scrovegni Chapel, however, as noted, that Justice alone is crowned, the virtue not of the poor but of the powerful. There is not a word in Dante of St Anthony, whose exploits are celebrated by Giotto. Both the father of Enrico Scrovegni and two members of the order of Cavalieri Gaudenti, to which Enrico belonged, are relegated to hell by Dante; the first as a miser, the others as hypocrites. Many such examples might be cited; the contrast between the two great Florentines seems to be irreconcilable.

What about the visual world of the Divine Comedy? On the one hand, we find in the Inferno an interest in nature similar to that of Giotto, though stress is laid almost entirely on obscene, caricatural and erotic characteristics; in other words, on the "comic," as the term was then understood. On the other hand, as regards Dante's treatment of the divine, certain elements are symbolic and strictly aniconic. Divinity presents itself to him in the form of light, as three circles of three colors; light and pure color, moreover, play an emblematic role of prime importance throughout the poem, in which the poet's tremendous powers of plastic description are almost exclusively applied to human beings, or rather to the bestial and vicious side of human beings.

In a sense, this comparison of Giotto and Dante, presupposing as it must a conflict rather than any kinship between them, turns wholly to Giotto's advantage. He was the more earthbound, the less mystical, the less medieval of the two; he was the man of the modern age. And with him painting regained its prestige with respect to literature. Not only did it stand now on an equal footing of dignity with poetry, but it began materially adding to man's knowledge of the world with a vividness and anecdotal verve worthy in every way of the contemporary *novella*; and, in addition to this, with a dramatic sweep, an earnestness of narration and a sustained intensity of feeling such as to compensate amply for the absence of tragedy in the literature of that day.

GIOTTO AND SIENESE PAINTING

The contrast between the Florentine school, founded by Giotto, and the Sienese school is an acknowledged fact, repeatedly attested to by the early historians and sharpened by the political conflict between the two cities. At Siena, as the Middle Ages drew to a close, there occurred not a cultural revolution but a transition which succeeded in preserving intact not only a large part of the medieval subject matter, but also the old function of the devotional image. A Madonna by Simone Martini, though rich in natural undertones, remains evocative and symbolic; the devout who approach it are emotionally affected by suavely harmonizing colors, by sensuous, intricately weaving lines, by the merging of real space into an atmosphere, if not spiritualized, anyhow highly sophisticated. Florentine painting, on the other hand, in the person of Giotto, set out to express the logical character of the world in its very essence. The image thereby assumed a sacred significance, because constructed in accordance with the rules of the physical universe, and also became an expression of the supreme principles of reality. While a Sienese Madonna conformed to the canons of elegance, of refinement, of sensuality and overt eroticism laid down by the court poetry of the period, a Florentine Madonna was born of intellectual speculations in geometry, perspective and proportions; it was a product of philosophy and mathematics combined. It too of course was symbolic, and in a sense more openly so than its Sienese counterpart. But it failed to cast an immediate spell over the beholder; it compelled him, rather, to meditation and scrutiny by slow degrees, to a critical and rationalistic attitude. From Petrarch we learn that "ignorant" people were incapable of appreciating it.

Giotto and the Florentines clearly anticipated what was to be the most typical characteristic of the Renaissance: rationalism, self-control, the struggle of reason against feeling, even at the risk of neglecting many aspects of human psychology and of giving rise to an intellectualism which in the end largely discredited itself. However, Giotto's concern with naturalistic details remains, for all their novelty, a factor of secondary importance (as does his irrepressible fondness for decoration): his object was to reduce the multiplicity of appearances to their ideal principles. The Sienese, on the other hand, worshipped God in the very multiplicity of phenomena and in external refinements; they gave painting the richness of goldsmiths' work and stained glass; they sought to put it within the reach of all classes of society by making it humane, anecdotal, pleasant to look at; in every object and living thing they recognized a value, rightfully conferred on it by the very fact of its existence, and they made no distinctions of hierarchy between individual and individual, between object and object. Sienese painting anticipated, not the Italian Renaissance, but the Northern Renaissance and Flemish painting. In another sense, it may be defined as candidly Franciscan, for it retained something of St Francis's warm sense of humanity.

Needless to say, the contrast which undoubtedly existed between Florentines and Sienese must not be pressed too far; historically speaking, there was never a radical divergence. The truth is that in many ways the Sienese school developed under the influence of Giotto and his followers. Some of the Sienese masters, the Lorenzetti for instance (who after all had worked in Florence) and even Duccio in his *Virgin and Child* at Badia ad Isola, often come very close to Giotto. As against this, we find Bernardo Daddi, one of Giotto's direct pupils, sharing the taste of the Sienese to a remarkable degree. What is more important to note is that the contrast between Siena and Florence only made itself felt gradually, especially after the rise and triumph of Simone Martini, so that the differences between the two schools may also be regarded as the natural result of a (perhaps) common spiritual evolution. Giotto himself, and this is the most human side of him, seems as time went on to have outgrown the heroic spirit of his younger days, and if more of his work had survived we might have reached the conclusion that, just as he succeeded in giving rise to a Sienese school of painting in opposition to his own, so he succeeded in nourishing it with ideas and in taking suggestions from it. Here again Giotto revealed himself as a universal artist.

WORKS

★

EARLY PAINTINGS · THE ASSISI FRESCOS
ROMAN WORKS · THE PADUA FRESCOS
WORKS AFTER PADUA

EARLY PAINTINGS

O F Giotto's youth we know next to nothing, nor do the early writers indicate any works which show him collaborating, as was customary at the time, with an older master. This is probably due to the fact that he was nearing thirty before he made a name for himself with his Assisi frescos, and above all with the Navicella mosaic in St Peter's at Rome, which, located in the first church of Christendom, became his most celebrated work, while the early paintings in Florence must have passed almost unnoticed.

Early writers, especially Florentines, insist on making Giotto a pupil of Cimabue; there is no documentary authority for this, but such historical and stylistic evidence as we have tells in favor of it. Vasari would have us believe that, as a poor shepherd boy, Giotto attracted the attention of Cimabue, who found him in the fields drawing sheep on a stone slab. But this is a mere legend. Circumstantial evidence suggests that Giotto received a good education, including literary studies, Boccaccio tells us, perhaps in the school attached to Santa Maria Novella.

Equally meager is our information about Cimabue himself, who was in Rome in 1272 and so presumably returned to Florence with firsthand experience of the classicistic taste then prevailing in Roman art circles. Quite possibly he met Arnolfo di Cambio in Rome. Cimabue's instruction or example must have been of fundamental importance to Giotto, even though he resolutely diverged from him and pursued a course almost violently opposed to that of his master. Speaking of Cimabue two centuries later, Cristoforo Landino praised him as the first to grasp "the natural features and the true proportions, which the Greeks called symmetry, and the figures which are dead in the earlier painters, he brought to life in varied attitudes." Important to note here is the allusion to structural solidity, obtained by the geometric quadrature of figures, a method known to us chiefly through the notebook of a slightly earlier French architect: Villard de Honnecourt. That Cimabue was also a qualified architect is shown by his collaboration with Arnolfo, toward the end of his career, in building the new cathedral of Florence.

The only painting that evinces a close personal contact with Cimabue happens to be Giotto's earliest known work: the large crucifix in Santa Maria Novella, still archaic in some respects but already the work of a master. It was designed to be hung, in the middle of the vast Dominican church, on a choir-screen which was torn down in 1500. Santa Maria Novella was the first great Gothic church of Florence, and also the most austere. Giotto's dramatic, profoundly moving crucifix was thus inserted in a rigorously severe architectural complex unrelieved by any decoration, in accordance with the ascetic principles observed in early monastic churches.

The history of the church itself provides a few clues to the dating of Giotto's crucifix. Beginning in 1279 with the apse, the building of the church went ahead slowly; the façade was not begun till 1300. But as early as 1285 the confraternity of the "Laudesi" ordered a large panel painting for their chapel in the transept: this was the famous *Madonna Enthroned* by Duccio, now in the Uffizi. Since the choir-screen from which Giotto's crucifix was to hang belonged to a later stage of construction, his painting may be assigned to a somewhat later date, to about 1290; even though the earliest records referring to it only go back to 1312.

Both Duccio and Giotto had close ties with Cimabue. It was only natural for the Dominicans to apply to them when new paintings were required, for Cimabue had already worked for the order, for which he made one of his masterpieces: the solemn crucifix in San Domenico at Arezzo, undoubtedly

CRUCIFIX: THE VIRGIN, C. 1290. ON WOOD.
SANTA MARIA NOVELLA, FLORENCE.

CRUCIFIX: ST JOHN, C. 1290. ON WOOD.
SANTA MARIA NOVELLA, FLORENCE.

the prototype of Giotto's, just as Cimabue's graceful *Madonna* in Santa Maria dei Servi at Bologna is the prototype of Duccio's. Circumstances suggest that in 1285 Cimabue was again absent from Florence, and that the Dominicans thereupon applied to his workshop for the *Madonna* and the crucifix they required. However this may be, it is certainly a tribute to the courageous modernism of the order, whose cultural influence must have been all-powerful at that time, that its Florentine church should have housed two such masterpieces, one marking the point of departure of the Sienese school, the other of the Florentine Renaissance. Duccio and Giotto, whose paths apparently never crossed again, were then living in the same quarter of Florence, each subjecting Cimabue's style to a severe critique of his own. Duccio was a few years older than Giotto, and the curve of his evolution as a painter was less dramatic; it neither forges ahead nor slackens off, but pursues the even tenor of its way, never falling short of the best standards of craftsmanship, and whatever was novel in his work was always novel in the subtlest, most intimate way. In his hands the sacred figures of the past were humanized, as if by a natural process of metamorphosis and attunement to the times; their gaze lost the sharp and chilling scrutiny of the Byzantines, and a mellow benevolence spread through their forms and features; they entered now, as it were, into a serene and confident relationship with the beholder. And when a touch of hardness or sternness lingered in the linear definition of forms, it was smoothed and softened by delicately blending colors.

In Giotto, beginning with the crucifix in Santa Maria Novella, the process was reversed. With him the human was deified, owing not so much to lofty refinements of style as to solid and tangible construction, calculated to produce the most compelling impression of physical force and presence. Giotto's conception of divinity was a subjective and dramatic one. And while Duccio fell heir to almost the whole of Cimabue's spiritual legacy, Giotto, for his part, gave a definitive catharsis to the religious and mystical torments he inherited from the past, transposing them from the emotional plane to a plane of rational certitude. Take the two half-length figures of the Virgin and St John, one at each extremity of the Santa Maria Novella crucifix: for the old gesture of despair, with the head pressed on the hand under an unbearable, crushing weight of anguish, is substituted the stoic forbearance of one who, dominating his grief with philosophic thoughtfulness, imposes a check upon himself. The same is true of the figure of Christ which, instead of slumping heavily to one side, with the belly swollen out, contorted with pain, hangs vertically from the fragile arms in a natural attitude of serene abandon, patterned almost certainly on the sculpture of the Pisanos.

Seen from close at hand, the huge crucifix reveals a number of highly interesting details in which we catch Giotto, at a decisive moment, breaking away from Cimabue. Here and there he kept to his master's practice, as in the sharp, flat, geometrized folds of the drapery, which forms a noticeable contrast with the soft sheen of the flesh tints, in spite of the bold mottling of the Virgin's mantle, with its rose-colored highlights, and the vibrant blue and violet-pink reflections on St John's mantle. Christ's body is carefully built up not on rhythmic but on geometric lines, with curves avoided wherever possible. Yet, the effect is one of extreme *morbidezza*, a delicacy and mellowness due chiefly to a skillful handling of color: over the green shadows of the body play roseate gleams whose articulation and vivacity are still strong today, even though the colors have darkened considerably in the intervening centuries. And the warm chestnut-brown of the hair and the reddish stubble of the beard, in contrast with the thick greenish shadows around and above the face, form a kind of aureole, more effective in its way than the traditional gilded one. The explicit stylization and gilded hatchings of Byzantine art have given way to an implicit, occult composition, an art that withholds its secrets, or better, its expedients. Gold is used very sparingly, and though gilding was originally intended in several places, it was in the end applied, very incompletely, only in the drapery and the borders of garments.

One further detail of significance: the outstretched arms are represented in perspective, with an eye to the effect produced by being seen from below. The faithful, passing under the crucifix and looking up, must have had the impression of a real body on a real cross, with their Savior's hand, torn by the nails, turned palm downwards as if to let the precious blood trickle down drop by drop.

Almost certainly earlier than the Assisi frescos is another, little known panel painting by Giotto, unfortunately mutilated: the *Virgin and Child* in the small monastic church of San Giorgio alla Costa, beyond the Arno, in Florence. The figures originally appeared in a much more spacious setting, the panel as it stands having been drastically cut down on both sides and at the bottom. Everything that in the crucifix at Santa Maria Novella was still a bold attempt at innovation, however fine the result poetically, has here become a serene and faultless achievement. The composition is radically simplified, and to this end the small size of the angels powerfully contributes. The full-bodied, almost statuesque plasticity of the Virgin serves to enhance her perfectly natural attitude. Untroubled by even the faintest hint of emotion, her face is a flawless oval, seen slightly from the side in order to suggest volume and to lend the figure a character at once human and hieratic. Even though the schematization of the angels' faces and the gracefully looped ribbons in their hair still stem from Cimabue, the two artists now have virtually nothing in common. Giotto seems, rather, to be confessing his debt to some sculptor's workshop presided over by a pupil of Nicola Pisano, perhaps Arnolfo di Cambio. The clean-cut lines of the Virgin's eye-sockets might have been made, one feels, by a sculptor's chisel.

Certain elements, the Cosmatesque decoration of the throne for example, and faint echoes of Cavallini, suggest that Giotto had already come in contact with Roman culture. Still, these might have reached him at second hand. The more we study this altar painting, the more we realize how much of Giotto's future career is implied in it; the early works of few artists have proved so truly prophetic.

ST FRANCIS GIVING HIS MANTLE TO A POOR MAN (DETAIL), 1296-1297.
FRESCO, UPPER CHURCH OF SAN FRANCESCO, ASSISI.

THE ASSISI FRESCOS

WHEN Giotto was called in (again, perhaps, on the strength of his being Cimabue's pupil) to paint the great fresco cycle devoted to St Francis in the Upper Church of San Francesco at Assisi, commissioned by the minister general of the order, Giovanni di Murro, elected in 1296 with the support of Pope Boniface VIII, he had completed his training and was an acknowledged master in his own right. Sacred art had surmounted the grave crisis brought on by the opposition of the early Franciscans to painted decorations, and the period of stagnation marked by the pontificate of Celestine V was past.

One of the most notable aspects of the pontificate of Boniface VIII, who as soon as he was elected hastened to grant indulgences to Assisi, was his policy of reviving the ancient pomp and pageantry of Rome, and for this he depended heavily on the figurative arts. His patronage of the arts was of course dictated by political considerations, for the conflict between Pope and Emperor over the rights and sovereignty of each had flared up again. Boniface, ardently embarked on a program of reconstructing and embellishing the Eternal City, was determined to establish himself as the only legitimate heir to the ancient empire of the Caesars. He resumed the practice—condemned by his enemies as idolatry—of having his portrait displayed in towns conquered by the papal troops, as a tangible sign of his authority, thus shrewdly taking advantage both of the enormous prestige then attaching to works of art exhibited in public and of the magic powers of actual presence popularly attributed to sculpture. The plasticity and dramatic imperiousness of Giotto's figures, indebted even in his early Florentine works to the principles of Roman classicism, were undoubtedly linked with the current belief in the magic properties of sculptured idols.

ST FRANCIS GIVING HIS MANTLE TO A POOR MAN, 1296-1297.
FRESCO, UPPER CHURCH OF SAN FRANCESCO, ASSISI.

There is no documentary evidence to show that Giotto
visited Rome before going to Assisi, but very probably he did.
At any event, it is now known for certain that the luxurious
decoration of the Franciscan basilica at Assisi was patronized

and financed by Rome, and carried out in strict compliance with the stipulations of the Roman Curia; it was largely the work of painters active at Rome; and Giotto's pictorial style and taste are steeped in obvious echoes of Rome. There is an undeniable connection between the architectural settings in his paintings and the contemporary or slightly earlier buildings designed by the Cosmati and by Arnolfo di Cambio. He seemed to be fascinated by those strictly proportioned but supremely elegant structures in which the sense of measure and balance, Cistercian in origin, unites with the grace, refinement and restraint of the classical tradition. So it comes as no surprise to find two unmistakable allusions to classical models: the sculpturesque pair of horses in the *Vision of the Fiery Chariot*, derived from some bronze equestrian group, like the famous bronze horses on the open gallery over the narthex of St Mark's in Venice; and, in the *Ordeal by Fire*, the group of priests of the Sultan of Babylon, closely patterned on a tetramorph. But, curiously enough, these reminiscences of the antique evoke a remote past, and serve exclusively to characterize either a celestial apparition or an exotic land of the East. Other references to ancient statues, marble reliefs and sculptured ornaments abound in these frescos, but they are always evocative rather than archeologizing; they show a firsthand knowledge of the style of ancient art, but a total indifference to the iconographical concepts of Greco-Roman antiquity. Much more precise, however, is the repertory of ancient motifs (ship, lighthouse, fisherman, and god of the winds) in the Navicella mosaic of 1298 in St Peter's, so the Assisi frescos must be earlier. At Assisi Giotto was still using these reminders of the classical world for fanciful and dramatic purposes. His impression of the antiquities he had seen in Rome affected only the style, not the iconography; this enabled him, however, to embody, freely and imaginatively, the suggestions offered by the ancients.

ST FRANCIS RENOUNCING THE WORLD (DETAIL), 1296-1297.
FRESCO, UPPER CHURCH OF SAN FRANCESCO, ASSISI.

To understand something of Giotto's intentions as he represented the events of St Francis's life, we must first of all note the use he made of this figurative repertory, which he had probably collected in his sketchbooks directly from nature. St Francis, as we learn from the biographies compiled by his immediate followers, freely chose to share the poverty and

◄ ST FRANCIS RENOUNCING THE WORLD (DETAIL), 1296-1297.
FRESCO, UPPER CHURCH OF SAN FRANCESCO, ASSISI.

hardships of the lowest classes of society and, by living humbly, to make poverty itself a moral quality. The events attending the life of humility he chose to lead took place, according to the early account—the *First Legend*—of Tommaso da Celano, in the bramble thickets of the Umbrian woods, in a wintry countryside devoid of shelter except for rude wayside inns. And while the beauties of nature are movingly hinted at, the idea of taking any delight in them is held at bay like a temptation of the devil. Indifference is shown to everything that comes under the heading of art or craftsmanship. The saint objected violently to the building of even the most modest convents, demolishing them with his own hands; instead of rebuilding abandoned churches, he merely patched them up.

Now in Giotto's frescos, from the very first scene (possibly not by his own hand, however), which has the Roman temple of Assisi in the background, St Francis appears in a setting that can only be described as monumental and aulic; relatively few scenes take place in the open country. The Cosmatesque repertory of architectural motifs, with its equivocal combination of ancient and modern, admirably serves to detach the episodes from the contemporary world, even while continually alluding to it, and to cushion the shock of the saint's poverty by evoking a remote and noble past.

This architectural setting is much more than a "stage property," for it plays what is in effect the leading role. It sets the mystical tone of the scenes; for example, when a voice comes from the crucifix of San Damiano and speaks to St Francis, our awareness of the miracle is heightened by the majestic ruins of the great basilica which fills the picture. It characterizes the background: the pontifical palaces, the magnificent triclinia of the Lateran, imperial courts, monastic chapter-houses. Even in the episodes of a bourgeois character, it qualifies the incident illustrated by lifting it from the secondary context, from the

ST FRANCIS RENOUNCING
THE WORLD AND THE DREAM OF
POPE INNOCENT III, 1296-1297.
FRESCOS, UPPER CHURCH OF
SAN FRANCESCO, ASSISI.

stormy background of communal life, and placing it in the current of contemporary political life. St Francis, in a word, was bodily assimilated to the highest social classes of his time, and made to seem what he never wished to be: an epic hero. And all this not by means of stylistic symbolism, but through an almost sunny clarity of exposition, which must have seemed extraordinarily lifelike at the time.

In the Padua frescos, once again, we find an abundant use of Cosmatesque elements, but with a substantial difference. The episodes illustrated at Padua were drawn from Holy Scripture and their architectural setting was designed to give them a historical character. The Assisi frescos dealt with a contemporary hero, and the setting had above all to make it clear that the *poverello* of Assisi was in reality a philosopher worthy of the ancients. This also accounts for the imaginative treatment of monuments which were familiar to everyone at the time, for example the church of Santa Chiara, which is given a splendid façade of inlaid marble, rivaling the one designed by Arnolfo for the cathedral of Florence—a background worthy of a king's funeral.

Turning from the backgrounds to the composition of individual scenes, and taking preferably the best of them, the least crowded and most spontaneously executed, we find the same monumentality and severity of expression. This novel method of composing could hardly be better described than in the following passage on classical rhetoric by Dionysius of Halicarnassus: "Such is the nature of austere composition. It requires that vocables should be firmly placed and set out, that they should take up strong positions, so that the lexical elements may be clearly seen and succeed one another at appropriate intervals separated by well-marked periods. No matter if frequent use is made of harsh, ill-sorted miscellanies, as in edifices built with squared stone, whose foundations

The rigorous structure governing all the scenes of the ▶ St Francis cycle is clearly brought out again in their simulated architectural cornices, painted with a precision and command of perspective that is quite amazing. As seen in photographs or with binoculars from the floor below, the simulated cornices with consoles above the scenes still succeed in deceiving the eye. This is the first recorded instance of a strict application of modern geometric perspective based on lines converging toward a single vanishing point. Giotto's contemporaries were therefore fully justified in praising him as a master of perspective. An equally impressive example of illusionism is to be found at Padua, in the simulated chapels in *trompe-l'œil* painted with consummate skill on either side of the large arch over the presbytery.

THE VISION OF THE FIERY CHARIOT
AND THE VISION
OF THE THRONES, 1296-1297.
FRESCOS, UPPER CHURCH
OF SAN FRANCESCO, ASSISI.

◀ Perspective came to be used by Renaissance artists not only as a technical but as a symbolical device to give unity to scenes, in much the same way as the canons of proportion were observed as a means of signifying that all the elements in the picture, whether human, architectonic or naturalistic, abided by a superior law. Giotto, as his style evolved, ended by closely approximating to this strict and absolute use of perspective and proportions; for example, in the last scenes painted at Padua and in those at Santa Croce in Florence. And the distance between this innovation of his and Cimabue's occasional bold applications of perspective is much greater than the distance separating him from Masaccio, Brunelleschi and Donatello—which goes to show again how surprisingly modern his vision of the world was.

consist neither of squared nor of polished stone, but often of rough stones thrown together pell-mell. It likes to unfold at length, sweeping along in grand phrases... It attends no less carefully to the members of the sentence, and chooses dignified and imposing rhythms. It does not demand that the members should be equal, or similar, or tied together in reciprocal bondage, but noble, simple, free. It aspires to be liker to nature than to art, and to depend on pathos more than ethos" (*De compositione verborum*, 147 r.). So with Giotto. The rhythm of the narrative is broad and sober, based on simple but energetic contrasts of both colors and attitudes. Every figure is self-significant and creates its own atmosphere, so that when it is surrounded by too many other figures the pictorial quality declines. Each movement and action echoes and re-echoes in space with almost magical potency. The saint's gesture as he offers his coat to a poor man (who will reveal himself as Christ); his uplifted arms, as he renounces his earthly possessions, in contrast to his father, who points to the ground; the exorcism of the demons afflicting the town of Arezzo; his prayer in a desolate wilderness, causing a spring to gush from the arid soil; the prophetic glance at his dying host, the knight of Celano; his attitude as he receives the stigmata; each is the focal point of the scene in which it occurs, and the rest is subordinated to it. But all this, as the above quotation from Dionysius of Halicarnassus shows, is the subtly calculated effect of skilled rhetorical procedures. The apparent simplicity of the work must have been little to the taste of the friars, as we divine from the steadily increasing number of figures in the scenes painted after Giotto's departure.

Giotto's style at this time exactly answered to the requirements of the great Roman patrons who had commissioned the work. The St Francis cycle in the Upper Church at Assisi was intended for the crowds of pilgrims, and indeed figured in precisely that part of the church which had been set aside for them, while the presbytery, decorated with apocalyptic scenes, was closed off by a choir-screen. It was not in the Church's interest to impress the idea of a pauper saint on the minds of these pilgrims, or worse, to picture him as the prophet of a social revolution; the important thing was to show that his behavior was wholly in keeping with the principles of the Roman court. The choice of episodes to be illustrated, all taken from the *Legenda Maior* of St Bonaventura, the official, canonically approved life of the saint, was almost exclusively designed to inculcate two ideas: that St Francis was endowed with miraculous powers, and that he kept in close and constant touch with the pope. The miracles illustrated by Giotto were chosen either because they had biblical parallels or because they proved his saintliness. But what is most surprising is that no works of mercy are included; instead of a benevolent and merciful saint, constantly succoring the poor and down-trodden, enfeebled though he was by fasting and penitence, we are shown a powerful, miracle-working saint whose efforts were bent entirely toward increasing the authority of the Church and promoting his order. As for the posthumous miracles (obviously intended to justify his beatification), they are concerned solely with men of rank or social distinction. The pilgrims saw in St Francis the promise of a better world. And Giotto portrayed him as the herald of a new age; but in a sense diametrically opposed to the spirit embodied by the saint himself, for he portrayed him as a model not of the mystical virtues but of the political virtues, of a religious force imposing morality from above. Everything in St Francis's personality had become keen-minded foresight, willpower, rationalism, unrelaxing self-control.

And if a wide gulf lay between the original rule of the order and the magnificent decorations lavished on the tomb of its founder, in the immense pilgrimage church erected to his

THE VISION OF THE FIERY CHARIOT (DETAIL), 1296-1297.
FRESCO, UPPER CHURCH OF SAN FRANCESCO, ASSISI.

memory, equally wide was the gulf between Cimabue's frescos
in the presbytery and Giotto's in the nave. Several scenes in the
presbytery devoted to St Peter and St Paul also allude to the
supremacy of Rome; but the tone, especially in the apocalyptic
subjects, is nevertheless inspired by an intimate religious fervor,
by a mysticism instinct with idealism, anguish and misgivings.
And the scenes from the Old and the New Testament, high
up between the windows of the well-lit nave, though impressive
in places for their aulic monumentality, maintain on the whole
the didactic tone of the old Benedictine cycles, from which much

THE EXPULSION OF THE DEMONS FROM AREZZO, DETAIL: THE TOWN,
1296-1297. FRESCO, UPPER CHURCH OF SAN FRANCESCO, ASSISI.

of their iconography derives. True, there is a close affinity between Giotto and the anonymous author of the scenes from the life of Isaac, with their exquisite symmetry and perspective, with their remarkable plasticity and, above all, their supreme distinction and elegance. Here, by general consent, we stand very close to the style and spirit of Giotto; all that is lacking is the firm, heroic, dramatic grasp which gives the Franciscan scenes a larger, more human dimension. So that even while acknowledging them to be the work of a very great Roman master (perhaps of Cavallini himself), one cannot help suspecting that it was Giotto who brought his influence to bear on them, and not vice versa. The same is true of the group of Passion scenes culminating in the *Lamentation over Christ*, which seems to post-date the beginning of the St Francis cycle and should be assigned, in our opinion, not to Giotto but to an artist close to Cimabue influenced by Giotto.

With Giotto's Assisi frescos, apocalyptic visions gave way to historical narrative, increasingly secular in tone. And instead of suggesting an unearthly world, painting now vied with sculpture in giving the illusion of actual physical presence, even in the smallest details. Could he have risen from the dead and seen these paintings, St Francis, it is safe to say, would have repudiated them as diabolic idols.

★

Did Giotto's style evolve in any way during the execution of the fresco cycle at Assisi? At first sight, the answer is yes, it evolved very noticeably. The scenes become more and more crowded and anecdotal; the colors, applied at first in sharp and elementary contrasts, grow more harmonious and lyrical; proportions are increasingly elongated; and the narrative, instead of hinging on a few leading figures, becomes sweeping, fluent, general. And all this before we reach the last three scenes,

THE ORDEAL BY FIRE BEFORE THE SULTAN, DETAIL: PRIESTS OF THE SULTAN,
1296-1297. FRESCO, UPPER CHURCH OF SAN FRANCESCO, ASSISI.

ST FRANCIS IN ECSTASY, 1296-1297.
FRESCO, UPPER CHURCH OF SAN FRANCESCO, ASSISI.

so graceful and dainty, so delicately colored, which, like the first of the cycle (presumably repainted), are attributable to an independent-minded follower of Giotto, akin to the anonymous author of an altarpiece in the Uffizi with St Cecilia and scenes of her life.

On the whole, however, the changes and innovations that occur as the work progressed are accompanied by an increasingly modest pictorial quality and by an increasingly incoherent composition. It has not yet been possible to single out the work of Giotto's collaborators, some of whom were interesting personalities. But a new study of the problem by Millard Meiss has been announced, based on an exact tabulation by the restorer Leonetto Tintori of each day's work on each individual fresco. Stylistic analysis shows, however, not only that Giotto's assistants were fairly numerous, but that large areas of the wall space, including some of the most famous scenes, were left to them. Giotto, probably owing to the brief period of time allotted him for the work, must have limited his personal contribution to a number of the leading figures, in some cases painting no more than the heads, while supervising as long as possible the general progress of the frescos, touching up and correcting the finished parts, and of course supplying designs, sketches, advice and help of all kinds. Without his guiding hand the results would never have been what they are, particularly as regards the skilled and coherent perspective of the initial scenes. What appeared, then, to be a marked evolution of his personal style may more plausibly be construed as a kind of reaction on the part of his pupils, who, lacking the moral and dramatic intensity of their master, developed above all the naturalistic and narrative possibilities of the new style.

The problem of distinguishing between Giotto's autograph work and what was executed on his designs or sketches presupposes another problem, and one of no mean order: that of determining the organization of his studio workshop or *bottega*, whose magnitude and complexity has been compared to that of the building yards of the great cathedrals. We may see a little more clearly into the problem by analyzing several of the scenes. In *St Francis giving his Mantle to a Poor Man*, Giotto himself must have executed both figures and closely supervised the laying in of the landscape, whose oblique lines adroitly serve to isolate and focus attention on the figure of St Francis. No doubt he also supplied sketches for the fine view of an Umbrian hill-town and for the monastery perched on the opposite hill; but he evidently left their execution entirely to his assistants. In *St Francis renouncing the World*, the hands of assistants are perceptible in the secondary figures, but the architecture is beautifully executed. In the *Dream of Pope Innocent III*, doubts arise as to the two figures, fine though they are, dozing beside the Pope's bed, while in the *Sanctioning of the Rules of the Order* perhaps only the figures of St Francis and the Pope were actually painted by Giotto. Handled with exquisite taste and balance are the *Vision of the Fiery Chariot* and the *Vision of the Thrones*. In the *Expulsion of the Demons from Arezzo*, the lovely view of the walled town, minutely depicted down to the rusticated stonework and decorative sculptures, with an almost Flemish love of detail, is the work of assistants; so are the small figures passing through the gates. While the stylization of the infidels in the *Ordeal by Fire* is very fine indeed, even though based on canons foreign to the master's taste, the whole right side of the scene, with the Sultan and his courtiers, is singularly uninspired. Many hands of varying ability can be detected in *Christmas Night at Greccio*, a scene too crowded and discursive; perhaps only one or two of the leading figures are Giotto's. Here his conception, however, is faithfully followed in the elegant rendering of the ambo, the pulpit, and the choir-screen with a crucifix seen from behind, all shown in flawless

ST FRANCIS PREACHING TO THE BIRDS, 1296-1297.
FRESCO, UPPER CHURCH OF SAN FRANCESCO, ASSISI.

perspective. Striking in their homogeneity, even if the secondary figures are the work of assistants, are the *Miracle of the Spring* and *St Francis preaching to the Birds*. The *Death of the Knight of Celano* conveys the impression of having been left unfinished; St Francis alone, rising to his feet behind the beautifully spread

THE MIRACLE OF THE SPRING (DETAIL), 1296-1297.
FRESCO, UPPER CHURCH OF SAN FRANCESCO, ASSISI.

THE DEATH OF THE KNIGHT OF CELANO (DETAIL), 1296-1297
(LATER REPAINTED). FRESCO, UPPER CHURCH OF SAN FRANCESCO, ASSISI.

table, seems to be by Giotto; the rest is more like a paraphrase of his manner than a faithful execution of his ideas. The same is true of the next scene, but to an even more marked degree; for this reason, and owing also to the intense, highly refined colors, it seems to belong to the group formed by the last three scenes, which are not by Giotto. Largely autograph in all likelihood, even though entrusted in part to pupils, is the *Apparition at Arles*, with its lovely transitions of color in the habits of the monks; also the scene of *St Francis receiving the Stigmata*, the last which Giotto supervised and unquestionably one of the finest and most coherent. As for the rest, he may have laid down the broad lines to be followed, but his pupils were left to their own devices, though availing themselves of a good many of Giotto's ideas and cartoons. The architectural settings now play no more than a decorative, picturesque role, while figures are elongated and their contours softened and blurred.

To explain these changes we can only suppose that Giotto was suddenly called away by other work more important than the frescos at Assisi. This, very probably, was the commission given him about 1298 by Cardinal Jacopo Stefaneschi, at the behest of the pope himself, for the Navicella mosaic in St Peter's. At Assisi not only did he leave the St Francis cycle unfinished (laboriously completed by his pupils as noted above), but also the decorations on the inner wall of the façade; here only the medallion with the Virgin and Child between two angels is Giotto's work.

To sum up, then. At Assisi Giotto's presence is felt above all in scenes with fewer figures; in those which were executed in fairly quick succession and thus betray no perceptible differences of manner. He seems to have executed personally—perhaps he was bound by contract to do so—only the leading figures, and carefully supervised the scenes which, iconographically, were most important. But as the work proceeded, his control over

THE APPARITION OF ST FRANCIS AT ARLES (DETAIL), 1296-1297.
FRESCO, UPPER CHURCH OF SAN FRANCESCO, ASSISI.

it lessened, finally disappearing altogether. Considering that the most confused und technically deficient group of frescos are those which come after the *Stigmata*, and in view of the controversy that raged before this miracle was officially recognized, it is by no means far-fetched to regard these theological difficulties as one possible reason for interrupting the work, which may not have been resumed till after 1304, the year in which the question was settled and the Church accepted the miracle of the Stigmata. But by this time Giotto was engaged elsewhere, and so the frescos were finished without him.

The presence of studio work, even in the scenes most closely supervised by Giotto, certainly detracts from the frescos; the style is in a sense roughened and hardened, and differs noticeably from that of his autograph works. Yet his assistants were anything but unskilled, and their archaizing style had one positive result. To the noble plasticity of the master they added a certain hardness of design which imparts to faces an element of religious transcendence. They thus pursued a traditional vision, as if the Middle Ages were not yet ended, and as if the new age of reason was not yet able to overcome the apocalyptic anguish and mysticism which had given Franciscanism its hold on the popular mind.

ROMAN WORKS

ALREADY at the end of the 13th century, Rome as it appeared to a visiting "tourist," as he rambled among impressive ruins, through fields still peopled with statues, with the guide to the "Mirabilia" in hand, and under the equally vivid impression of the new impetus then being given to architecture and the plastic arts, must have been very different from the image of the city that became typical for anyone who had lived there a long time. Even today those who visit Rome and those who live there take a fundamentally different attitude to the city. Antiquity, for the first, is an inspiration and an ideal; it is like recovering a patrimony of lost experience which one had unconsciously yearned for; like a re-immersion in an atmosphere of superior wisdom and, above all, of more generous morality with respect to the ideological restrictions of Christianity. But the enthusiasm of those who live there allows itself at length to be stifled by the weight of tradition and by indifference to any possibility of renewal. This is the Rome, rotten with millenary evils, which holds out no hope of any real solution, but aims always at a compromise between idealism and reality, between indulgence and severity.

Summoned to Rome to execute the Navicella mosaic, fresh from the burning atmosphere of Franciscanism, and plunged into the midst of the intrigues and cosmopolitan worldliness of the Roman Curia, did Giotto too feel the need to soften and smooth his style? Such would seem to have been the case, but no certitude is possible of course without the works actually done in Rome, and these, unfortunately, have nearly all disappeared. An inventory of the lost works, based on documentary evidence, forms an impressive list: the Navicella in the atrium of St Peter's, entirely restored; the frescos decorating the Loggia delle Benedizioni in the old basilica of the Lateran, of which only a fragment survives; various decorations, among them a *Virgin and Child*, all destroyed when Old St Peter's was torn down; other paintings described as *"pannus cum figuris Jotti inseratus et rotolatus,"* as *"imago manu Jotti in panno linteo posita in quodam ligno concavo,"* of which we can form no idea whatever; as for the polyptych in the Vatican Pinacoteca, commissioned by Cardinal Stefaneschi, it is almost entirely the work of pupils. With the help of literary sources and a few old copies, however, we can imagine what some of these were like.

The mosaic representing the ship (i.e. the "Navicella") of the Apostles caught in a storm on the Sea of Galilee (Matthew, XIV), with St Peter walking on the waters toward Christ, was for long Giotto's most celebrated work. According to a document published by Mancini in the 17th century, whose authenticity there is no reason to doubt, it was commissioned about 1298 by Cardinal Jacopo Stefaneschi, nephew of Pope Boniface VIII and a canon of St Peter's, with a view to attracting the attention of pilgrims, whose traditional practice it was, upon entering the atrium of the basilica, to turn to the east and kneel in adoration of the sun. This custom had already been denounced in a Bull issued by Pope Leo I in the 5th century; but evidently, though over eight hundred years had passed since then, this avatar of paganism had by no means disappeared. Shrewdly hitting on a realistic-minded solution, Cardinal Stefaneschi had the great mosaic put up, thereby converting the superstitious practice into an act of devotion.

Hence the location and unusual isolation of the work; a word now in explanation of its iconography. That it is meant to glorify the Roman Church is obvious: the storm-tossed ship, according to St Matthew, symbolizes the eternal struggle and eternal salvation of the Church and of those who seek shelter in its bosom. Yet, in view of the bitter political conflict then raging between Pope and Emperor, we realize that the Navicella mosaic

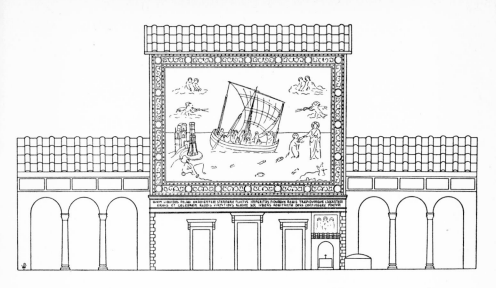

LOCATION OF THE "NAVICELLA" MOSAIC IN THE ATRIUM OF ST PETER'S.
(FROM THE DRAWING BY W. PAESELER)

very definitely re-echoes the polemics of the day. According to a work written at the court of Boniface VIII, the storm threatening "not only the pope and the cardinals... but all the passengers in the ship of the Church," was stirred up by the "multitude of wild beasts," i.e. by the secular princes. The metaphor of the ship, the "navicella," also occurs in the writings of those who defended the imperial authority. Alexander of Roes had written a few years before: "Just as the Roman eagle cannot fly with but one wing, so too the little ship of St Peter cannot be steered with a single oar through the tempests and whirlwinds of this century." In other words, Emperor and Pope should join forces for the moral guidance of humanity. Boniface himself, however, saw things differently: a single "vicarius Christi" sufficed and he was that man. And this was figuratively signified in Giotto's mosaic: St Peter's boat has but a single oar and it is held by St Paul, the Roman Apostle *par excellence.*

The impression produced by this powerfully realistic mosaic is attested by the following incident, among others. When St Catherine of Siena knelt at the foot of Giotto's "Navicella," at a time when both St Peter's and Rome (abandoned by the papacy for Avignon) had entered on a decline, at the thought that upon her alone had fallen the task of guiding the heavy oar of the ship of the Church, spasms ran through her limbs to which she remained subject for the rest of her life.

The Navicella must have been the work into which Giotto put the best of himself. Studying copies of it, in particular a 17th-century copy (Museo di San Pietro, Rome) reproducing it faithfully except for the figure of St Peter, apparently restored in the 16th century, one is struck by the parallel between Giotto and Roman and Christian antiquity. This, undoubtedly, was due in part to the intervention, probably fairly strenuous, of Cardinal Stefaneschi himself, one of the outstanding members of the cultural élite of the time, who was also closely connected with Cavallini. But naturally Giotto's own innovations are most striking of all: the use of vivid colors, still bright in spite of the unfortunate 17th-century recasting of the work; the many foreshortenings; the monumentality and plasticity of the composition. Early writers extol the variety of gestures, and their fine accordance with each personage and the dramatic part he plays in the episode; whereas the impression we get now is rather one of a certain confusion in the grouping of figures.

On the strength of a 17th-century epigraph, it is usually assumed that three mosaic medallions with half-length angels belonged to the Navicella. One of these was removed to the church of San Pietro at Boville Ernica, near Frosinone, while two remain at Rome in the Grotte Vaticane; one of the latter,

HALF-LENGTH ANGEL, 1298-1300. MOSAIC MEDALLION FROM ST PETER'S.
GROTTE VATICANE, ROME.

unfortunately, has been altogether restored. But a 16th-century print shows that the decorative elements framing the Navicella mosaic consisted only of plant-forms. Were these medallions

POLYPTYCH FROM THE BADIA: ST JOHN (FRAGMENT), C. 1301-1302.
UFFIZI, FLORENCE.

POLYPTYCH FROM THE BADIA: ST BENEDICT (FRAGMENT), C. 1301-1302.
UFFIZI, FLORENCE.

then placed beneath the mosaic, beside an inscription? The most plausible hypothesis is that they figured on the inner wall of the façade, which was decorated with a band of similar medallions.

These medallions keep to the aulic classicism of the Navicella mosaic, though their plastic energy is less violent. Forcibly but serenely presented, the angels are distinguished by a certain Hellenizing grace, which suggests a firsthand knowledge not only of the painting of contemporary Rome, but of that of early medieval Rome.

Early sources mention, among other works executed for St Peter's, a cycle of five large-scale frescos in the apse. What appears to be a much repainted fragment of this (now in the Fiumi Collection, Assisi) was published by Adolfo and Lionello Venturi. It represents two half-length apostles with an unusual mildness of expression. There is something in common here, it seems to us, with the mood of lyrical melancholy pervading the Uffizi polyptych of about 1301-1302 which, as Procacci has shown, comes from the Badia in Florence. This too is a work of great mildness and refinement; the figure of the Virgin, though more monumental, anticipates the tenderest of Sienese icons.

Only a fragment survives of the last work executed by Giotto in Rome: the great fresco cycle for the loggia of St John Lateran, representing Boniface VIII promulgating the Jubilee of 1300, the baptism of Constantine (the Emperor submitting to the Pope!), and the founding of the Lateran basilica.

Again we have a courtly work intended to glorify the Church. The iconographic prototype of the central scene has been identified by C. Mitchell as a bas-relief representing the Emperor Theodosius in the tribune of his palace in Constantinople. Boniface VIII, portrayed in the act of promulgating the Jubilee, is meant to represent not so much a spiritual guide as the foremost political authority of the world, the rightful heir of those Emperors whose prerogatives he sought to revive.

He steps forward not merely to promulgate an act of clemency, but to proclaim a law worthy of eternal commemoration. And distinguishable among his audience is a crowned monarch. The overweening pride of the ambitious pontiff is seen again in the frequent repetition of the armorial bearings of his family.

It would be difficult to imagine a more solemn theme than this. Yet, judging by the extant autograph fragment and by Grimaldi's copy in color of the original, Giotto seems to have evaded the implications of the theme. His dramatic ardor has very noticeably cooled, as compared with what it was at Assisi. He tends to linger over details and anecdotal elements; so true is this that in the three central figures, Boniface VIII, the cleric holding up the roll, and the dignitary traditionally identified as Cardinal Caetani, what impresses itself upon us is not so much the ceremonious solemnity of the occasion as the shrewd characterization of facial features, carried to the point of sharply individualized portraits. The portrayal of the crowd below must have produced a dazzling effect, with its wealth of vivid colors and striking contrasts.

How are we to account for these changes of style? It is unfortunate that we still know so little of the Rome of that day, which must have been an extremely stimulating melting pot of all the currents and cross-currents of contemporary art, both in and out of Italy. And if Philip the Fair came to Rome in search of the artists he needed in France, it is equally true that he brought French artists with him to Rome—the famous portraitist Etienne d'Auxerre, for example. The penetration of French literary culture, moreover, was such as to make itself felt in the domain of the figurative arts. Giotto's evolution certainly suggests that, even before Philip's humiliating triumph over the Pope at Anagni in 1303, the political-minded classicism of Boniface VIII had come to seem—in Giotto's eyes at least—a whimsical and anachronistic dream.

THE LAST JUDGMENT (FRAGMENT), 1304. FRESCO ON THE INNER WALL
OF THE FAÇADE, SCROVEGNI CHAPEL, PADUA.

THE PADUA FRESCOS

THE frescos in the Scrovegni Chapel at Padua are Giotto's next documented work, following his stay in Rome; they date, as we shall see, from 1304 to 1306. Nothing is known for certain of his activities or whereabouts in the intermediate years, but one or two inferences may be drawn.

Giotto must have left Rome in 1303 at the latest, perhaps as a result of the grave political disorders culminating in the tragic death of Boniface VIII in 1303; possibly he had already left the city by the end of 1300, when he finished the Jubilee fresco, and may then have returned for a time to Florence. In 1303 Giovanni di Murro, who had previously commissioned the Assisi frescos, returned to Italy from abroad and was appointed Bishop of Porto. It seems probable that, thanks to him, Giotto was again summoned by the Franciscans, not to Assisi, where there were disturbing repercussions of the Roman crisis, but to Rimini. There, in the Franciscan church which later, as renovated by Leon Battista Alberti, became the famous Tempio Malatestiano, he painted scenes of the life of St Anthony (now lost) and, almost certainly with his assistants, the great crucifix still pre-served there. Then he went to Padua. Such, according to the chronicler Riccobaldo Ferrarese, is the sequence of Giotto's Franciscan cycles—Assisi, Rimini, Padua, and this seems plau-sible enough. The Rimini crucifix, above all in the molding, recently rediscovered by F. Zeri, still shows a close connection with the Roman art world, and in particular with the Stefaneschi polyptych (as does the School of Rimini, which sprang from Giotto). Then, very probably, Enrico Scrovegni took advantage of the presence of Giotto and his studio in Padua to entrust him with the decoration of the Arena Chapel.

Since the evolution of an artist's style depends not only on the force of his genius, but on the opportunities and working conditions offered him, it is only natural that the Padua frescos should differ very noticeably from those at Assisi and Rome, and even from the polyptych of the Florentine Badia, datable to immediately after his departure from Rome. Unfortunately no copy or sketch remains of the lost frescos at Rimini and in the Santo at Padua. So that we can only look to Paduan culture, and to reflections of it traceable in his work, for some explanation of the new development of Giotto's painting.

Because it adjoined the luxurious palace built by Enrico Scrovegni on the ruins of a Roman amphitheater, the Arena Chapel is usually assumed to have been his private chapel. But this is not quite the truth of the matter. Actually it served as the church of one of the principal religious orders of that day, the Cavalieri Gaudenti ("mirthful knights"), and was designed to accommodate their assemblies. Their refectory, partially filled in, still exists below ground level. Records dating back to 1277 mention legacies and gifts of money and material for the construction of the building. To Enrico Scrovegni, a knight of the order of the Gaudenti, goes the credit for initiating the work of construction on a large scale and seeing it through.

His own attitude is, in a sense, quite as ambiguous as that of the order to which he belonged, but it must have tallied by and large with Giotto's interpretation, on the walls of the chapel, of the lives of Christ and the Virgin.

Enrico was the son of Reginaldo Scrovegni, whom Dante consigned to the seventh circle of his Inferno as a usurer. As such, usury being a mortal sin, he was debarred from confession while living and from burial in consecrated ground when dead; and the Church as a rule was strict in these matters. The son, in these circumstances, had no right to inherit his father's estate. But in this case a compromise—the more necessary as the Scrovegnis were then very unpopular in Padua—was reached

THE LAST JUDGMENT, DETAIL: THE VIRGIN AND ANGELS, 1304.
FRESCO, SCROVEGNI CHAPEL, PADUA.

either by Reginaldo before his death (but then Dante would have had no reason to put him in Hell) or more probably by Enrico, thanks to his personal friendship with the future Benedict XI. The terms were hard: Enrico was bound to enter the lay order of the Cavalieri Gaudenti, which meant that he had to make over any illicit or ill-gotten gains, even if inherited, to the jurisdiction of the local bishop. He was further enjoined to renovate the Arena Chapel at his own expense, to distribute alms with the utmost largess, and to lead a retired life; but in exchange he was granted permission to build himself a fine palace and to inherit a substantial share of his father's estate.

It is difficult to say how far his contrition and piety as a church builder were sincere. There is evidence both for and against him. In his favor are the rather touching inscriptions (drawn up by Scrovegni himself) and his express desire to be interred in the church he had built, this perhaps to obviate any risk of the non-Christian burial that had befallen his father. Against him may be reckoned, first, the distrustful attitude of both the bishop and the Augustinians (i.e. the Eremitani), who were entrusted with the spiritual guidance of the Cavalieri Gaudenti, and therefore of Enrico Scrovegni too; secondly, the very splendor of the church itself, which seems to have been intended above all to glorify his own family; and lastly the personal vicissitudes of Scrovegni himself, who was shortly afterwards driven into exile at Venice by the implacable hatred of his fellow citizens. Scardeone, a local chronicler, accuses Enrico of being weak-willed, abject and incapable of defending his own wealth and property. The same equivocal behavior seems to have characterized the Cavalieri Gaudenti, who at that time had already lost sight of their original purpose of rooting out heresy, and whom Dante brands as hypocrites and misers, covetous and unjust. True, the members of this order (or rather those who were compelled to join it) ostensibly led a frugal life and renounced public office; but in actual practice they moved in the highest social circles (only aristocrats were admitted to the order) and finally came to form quite a powerful caste, capable of exerting a political influence beyond that of the factions.

A perusal of the documents relating to the Chapel and the order may help to clarify the evolution of Giotto's style at Padua.

In 1300, empowered to make use of his father's wealth for stipulated purposes, Enrico Scrovegni bought the ground on which the Roman Arena had stood, and prepared to build a palace and a chapel. For this he soon obtained permission from Bishop Ottobono dei Razzi and in March 1304 the chapel was dedicated to the Virgin. Had it been wholly completed by that date? We know that it had not; only the present nave was finished. This can be inferred from a petition of January 1305, in which the chapter of the Eremitani (whose duty it was, as we have said, to keep an eye on the Cavalieri Gaudenti) complained that Enrico Scrovegni was having a bell-tower built beside the new church, to the great prejudice of the friars, who thus stood in danger of losing their exclusive prerogative (and source of a steady income in the form of offerings) of publicly calling the faithful to worship. In their petition they make much of the fact that the permission granted Scrovegni provided only for a small church, a mere oratory, for himself, his wife, mother and family, with no provision for public worship; whereas now, in view of the new work getting under way, the edifice bade fair to become a large church. Besides the bell-tower, presumably, Scrovegni had a small portico added in front (torn down in the 19th century) and must have been planning an annex to the chapel, as may be deduced from the presence of a door on the righthand side, which had to be walled up before Giotto could paint the allegorical figure of Charity which now covers it. Neither bell-tower nor portico nor this door figures in the accurate and detailed picture of the chapel which we see in the fresco of the

Last Judgment on the inner wall of the facade, above the main entrance, showing young Scrovegni offering the chapel to the Virgin, accompanied by St John and an unspecified female saint.

Now while there can be no doubt that the protest of the Eremitani was directed against Scrovegni's decision to transform his private chapel into the mother church of the order to which he belonged (encouraged in this, apparently, by indulgences obtained in 1302 *"pro visitantibus ecclesiam"* and above all by the papal Bull of March 1, 1304), the fact remains that Giotto's pictured model of the chapel in the *Last Judgment* faithfully represents it as originally planned, without either bell-tower or portico; so this fresco must date from before January 1305. That the fresco decorations of the chapel were not only begun but pretty well advanced at that time is confirmed by another complaint lodged against Scrovegni by the Eremitani, charging him with "many things done for show, out of pride and self-interest, rather than for the glory and honor of God; things he is again doing and preparing to do, without the Bishop's permission." Architecturally, however, the chapel is simplicity itself. What is referred to here can only be Giotto's frescos; nor is it at all surprising, in view of the then prevailing hostility of the religious orders to paintings and decorations, to find them condemned out of hand as vain and superfluous. The most zealous faction of the Franciscan order, the so-called Spirituals, passed exactly the same judgment on the Assisi frescos. With the Padua frescos, then, Giotto not only renewed religious painting but restored it to its place in the office of divine worship. And again, as he had done at Rimini, he created a school.

A few other inferences can be drawn from these documents. As the Eremitani wielded a certain influence and were the authorized superiors of the Cavalieri Gaudenti, no doubt their protest was not lodged in vain. The Bishop must have remonstrated severely with Scrovegni, and while he did not go so far as

THE LAST JUDGMENT, DETAIL: HELL, 1304.
FRESCO, SCROVEGNI CHAPEL, PADUA.

to have the campanile dismantled (it is still visible in modern prints), he restrained Scrovegni's mania for building and evidently forbade him to enlarge on the original plans of the chapel or even to carry them out completely. In Giotto's pictured model of it, which otherwise reproduces all its parts exactly as they exist today, we find a projecting transept with tall windows (therefore not a sacristy). But the transept was never actually

THE LAST JUDGMENT, DETAIL: HELL, 1304.
FRESCO, SCROVEGNI CHAPEL, PADUA.

Gi. 26

built. How keenly this was regretted is shown by the fact that
some compensation for it was sought and found in the shape of
two simulated side chapels, painted with the utmost realism, in
illusionist perspective, on either side of the great arch closing the
nave. The simulated chapels conform to the original building
plans, and their windows are of the same type; each chapel was
to have an altar and, as we see from the painted perspectives,
was to be frescoed, like the nave.

By order of the Bishop, then, the work was brought rapidly to a close, provisionally anyhow, and the church was officially consecrated on March 6, 1306. For the occasion Scrovegni received the loan of some tapestries from the basilica of St Mark's in Venice. Some part of the decoration must have been incomplete and these were needed to replace it. What had not yet been painted were evidently the scenes from the life of the Virgin, in the apse, which were not made till much later; that is, the *Death*, *Coronation* and *Assumption of the Virgin*. Indeed, though the Arena Chapel was dedicated to the Virgin, the scenes devoted to her form a very limited part of the whole and were relegated—except for those in the apse—to the upper tier. We get the distinct impression that the scenes from her life were only introduced as an expedient or afterthought. This impression deepens into a conviction when we observe that this cycle of scenes infringes on the lower part of the barrel vault and fails to fit coherently into a decorative system obviously planned before they were painted. There are inconsistencies in its iconography; it even happens that episodes of the same scene are repeated, as Arslan pointed out as far back as 1923.

This last observation clears up the chronology of the frescos. First of all, the master painted the *Last Judgment*, on the inner wall of the facade, finished well before January 1305, in which we see the model of the chapel as originally planned; by the same date the scenes of the life of Christ were already well advanced; then, when the Bishop's decision was announced, the work was hastily brought to a close for the time being, before the single apsidal chapel had been built. Now that it was forbidden to build the transept, where an immense wall space was to be reserved for a fresco cycle devoted to the Virgin and Joachim, Giotto was forced to add a few scenes of her life high up on the side walls of the nave, above the stories of Christ, and, as a last expedient, to add an *Annunciation* on the triumphal arch. It was then planned to devote the walls of the apsidal chapel to the final scenes of the Virgin's life. But by the time this chapel was built, or completed, Giotto had left Padua; it was ultimately decorated by a pupil or follower. The stories of Joachim and the childhood of the Virgin (these were the scenes added at the last minute on the upper register of the side walls) may be dated to between January 1305 and March 1306. The chronological sequence of the frescos is thus as follows: *Last Judgment* (1304), *Scenes from the Life of Christ* (largely before January 1305), *Stories of Joachim and the Virgin* (between January 1305 and March 1306).

The chronology here proposed, based on a fresh analysis of the documents and the architecture of the building, corresponds very well with the general development of the style. The influence exerted on Giotto by Rome, and by Cavallini in particular, is chiefly, indeed almost exclusively visible in the *Last Judgment* on the inner wall of the façade: a work in many ways ill-balanced, imperfectly organized around a troublesome three-light window. But since its iconography was prescribed by tradition, it better enables us to analyze the emergence of Giotto's new poetics as they took form in Padua.

Precisely because we find ourselves in the presence of what is, judged by the highest standards, almost an artistic failure, we can accept Gnudi's general assessment of the work: "For Giotto the Last Judgment, Hell and Paradise remain a supernal world unindividualized in its poetic reality... which only intermittently, in this or that detail, is lit up with poetic truth." But how are we to account for its being a relative failure? That it should be so is the more surprising when we realize that, however limited in scope, the autograph parts of the *Last Judgment* are perhaps more numerous than in the other frescos in the chapel, whose apparent homogeneity was only obtained by the most skillful supervision and coordination.

LIFE OF CHRIST: THE NATIVITY (DETAIL), 1304-1305.
FRESCO, SCROVEGNI CHAPEL, PADUA.

Before analyzing the style, it may be well to give a brief description of the huge fresco. At the top of the wall, one on either side, two angels of the Apocalypse unfurl the heavens, which are symbolized by sun and moon (one angel is reproduced on page 8 of this book). Beneath them, still flanking the large window, come the serried ranks of the angelic hosts with their banners. In the center, between the twelve Apostles, each seated on his separate throne like the judges of antiquity, is Christ in a mandorla upheld by angels, leaning slightly toward the procession of the Elect led (and this is unusual) by the Virgin, while on His left (to our right) opens the yawning abyss of Hell. Beneath Christ is the Cross, held by two angels; behind it, at the base, a small figure, one of the Damned, is trying to hide. A little lower comes the scene of the chapel's dedication, with the famous but rather uninspired portrait of Enrico Scrovegni. Though it keeps in the main to set formulas, the iconographical scheme seems to derive in particular from Cavallini's similar *Last Judgment* in Santa Cecilia in Rome. A few details, on the other hand, are taken from the mosaic representing the same subject in the cupola of the Baptistery in Florence, but Giotto naturally recast them in a thoroughly modern style.

The comparison with these prototypes shows clearly what Giotto's intentions were—and also what his limitations were, anyhow at this early stage of the work. First of all, he deliberately eliminated every symbolic and abstract mode of expression. The portrayal of the divine figures is substantially naturalistic; they are only distinguished from the others by their larger size. This is strikingly evident in the respective proportions of the Elect and the angels escorting them; only their haloes and size distinguish the second from the first. Even more surprising (and obviously intentional) are the identical proportions of Enrico Scrovegni and the Virgin: were the latter

LIFE OF CHRIST: THE PRESENTATION IN THE TEMPLE, 1304-1305.
FRESCO, SCROVEGNI CHAPEL, PADUA.

not standing slightly above ground level, she would appear
thoroughly human; her hands are so close to Scrovegni's
moreover, the direct contact between them is so manifest,
that little or no distinction remains between human and divine.

While a rich background or undercurrent of symbolism was set up in Cavallini's work by a majestic presentation and incisive linework, in Giotto's Assisi frescos by the monumental heroism of the figures, in Byzantine art by distortion and insistent rhythms, all this is lacking at Padua. With the result that the figures in the *Last Judgment* have a curious ambiguity, almost as if Giotto could not quite bring himself to believe in the transcendence of the divine. The repetition of faces and the distribution of the scene into well-marked zones, devoid now of any abstract rhythm to lend them dramatic tension or symbolic overtones, are seen for what they are: decorative expedients, often rather tedious. The only notable characteristic of these figures is, at best, their serene elegance. Yet their naturalism is not such as to transpose the scene, thus deprived of any sense of the sacred, to the earthly plane and humanize it.

The absence of any real dramatic sense is especially notice-able in the figures of the Damned, for all the extraordinary novelty of their naturalism, already Late Gothic in spirit; but at the same time they are curiously barren of human warmth. They fail to arouse either terror or sympathy. What they do reveal, however, is an anecdotal verve worthy of a great story-teller. Animated by strange moral principles, they seem at times to give violent expression to anticlerical sentiments, as in the episode of a bishop selling a false indulgence to a sinner. The alternately obscene and macabre incidents taking place in this inferno, so different from Dante's, mark the furthest limit of Giotto's naturalism. Yet there are thoroughly modern touches that come like glimpses of the future. The figure of the hanged man, with his belly torn open and his intestines spilling out, is an almost textual anticipation of the macabre taste and very worldly uneasiness of Pisanello. At times, on the other hand, we find combinations of images that almost smack of Surrealism, like the reclining female nude tormented by demons, in which the theme of lust combines with the Freudian theme of blood—in this case, the blood of Christ. This, perhaps, is the first real female nude in the history of European art, for ancient sculptures, of the Hermaphrodite type, were still to be used as models for such subjects for a long time to come. But this nude of Giotto's at Padua is undoubtedly based on a flesh-and-blood model; there is nothing literary about the current of eroticism that emanates from her.

This is not to say that these parts of the fresco are necessarily by Giotto's own hand. But the very fact that they are there proves that he sanctioned them.

What had been a defect in the *Last Judgment*, which called for an epic, apocalyptic tone, became an extraordinary lyrical quality in the scenes from the life of Christ. The figure of the Savior, at Padua, is sweetly and lyrically humanized; indeed, throughout the narration of his earthly life, each scene has a character of its own, idyllic, lyrical, moving or dramatic as the case may be. An unfailing cohesion of style and content is perhaps the supreme novelty of this fresco cycle. The sacred figures remain of course strongly idealized but, unlike those at Assisi, they are nevertheless imbued with a vibrant humanity. The events in which they take part unfold on a psychological plane parallel to that of daily life. And the ambiguity that dissipated the dramatic power of the *Last Judgment* here heightens it, for the co-existence in Christ of a psychology at once human and divine underlies the very theme of the Gospel. It might even be said that the spirit of the Padua frescos is peculiarly suited to the devotional outlook of the Latin peoples; incapable of arriving at a theological interpretation of the Gospel, and by its very nature debarred from attaining to the abstract idea of God, the Latin mind fixes on the humanity of the Son.

LIFE OF CHRIST: THE PRESENTATION IN THE TEMPLE (DETAIL), 1304-1305.
FRESCO, SCROVEGNI CHAPEL, PADUA.

Was Giotto's spiritual attitude, in these initial scenes, in part determined by his environment at the time? Probably it was. To my knowledge, no studies of the forms of worship peculiar to the Cavalieri Gaudenti exist, but we know that they emerged and developed in the lyrical climate of the late medieval *"laudi,"* the first examples of dramatic verse in the vulgar tongue of Italy and still closely connected with the liturgy. The name of the order ("mirthful knights") suggests a "courtly" type of worship, conditioned by the aristocratic world of Provençal poetry, with its equivocal combination of the erotic and the mystical. Even in the lyrics of Giotto's time, the knight's beloved is often likened to the Virgin, sometimes even identified with her; and always revered with expressions of devotion closely akin to those of Christian worship. Love is defined as a sacred cult, a path to the spiritual life. And, conversely, the cult of the Virgin assumes a tone of affectionate familiarity, taking place in a climate undisguisedly amorous which, while contributing to an accord far more intense and intimate than before between the devotional image and the worshipper, also deprives the divine of its hieratic and eschatological aspect. What we are accustomed to define as the mystical currents of the late Middle Ages are all, in reality, sharp psychological reactions against transcendence. One is reminded, in this context, of a sonnet in praise of his beloved by a contemporary of Giotto, Guido Cavalcanti, whom Boccaccio defined as a "natural philosopher," like Giotto, and whom he described as intent on seeking "to find if it might be that God is not." In the sonnet I have in mind (the one beginning *"Una figura della donna mia..."*), the poet's beloved is likened to a sacred image in Orsanmichele in a way that amounts to a total identification, for all the miracles described in the poem, divine or amatory, are the effect and result of a supreme force, Love.

This vein of courtly poetry, re-echoing medieval mysticism in its love of precious colors, its decorative richness, its otherworldly idealization, was exploited to the full a decade later by Simone Martini, to unsurpassable effect. But Giotto, instead of sublimating sacred figures, confined himself to softening and chastening them, and for the first time in the history of religious art brought them down to earth.

LIFE OF CHRIST: THE FLIGHT INTO EGYPT (DETAIL), 1304-1305.
FRESCO, SCROVEGNI CHAPEL, PADUA.

LIFE OF CHRIST: THE MASSACRE OF THE INNOCENTS (DETAIL), 1304-1305.
FRESCO, SCROVEGNI CHAPEL, PADUA.

This is particularly noticeable in their attitudes and gestures; these have nothing sacramental about them, but are patterned on the habits of daily life, though rendered with a certain reticence and solemnity. The question thus arises, to what extent Giotto may have drawn on the sacred drama for his transposition of the divine into terms of everyday life. In the churchyard of the Arena Chapel (for, in spite of ecclesiastical prohibition, public spectacles continued to be held throughout the Middle Ages at the same places where the ancients had held them) the Easter mystery of the Annunciation was acted each year. This, however, must have been a particularly elementary type of play, and in general the so-called *"laude,"* acted in the vernacular tongue, is considered to have been still in the

LIFE OF CHRIST: THE ENTRY INTO JERUSALEM (DETAIL), 1304-1305.
FRESCO, SCROVEGNI CHAPEL, PADUA.

LIFE OF CHRIST: THE WASHING OF FEET (DETAIL), 1304-1305.
FRESCO, SCROVEGNI CHAPEL, PADUA.

embryonic state at that time. But magnificent pageants were being staged in Italian towns, at Padua in particular; and at Padua too Albertino Mussato, with his *Ecerinide*, was reviving classical tragedy.

A comparison of Giotto and Mussato would carry us too far afield here. Suffice it to say that, in addition to their common desire to give not symbolic but vividly realistic representations of historical, political and biblical episodes, they both developed a new and remarkable capacity for bringing out the opposing forces of the drama and for presenting it not in terms of a general rhetorical atmosphere, but as a concrete encounter or conflict of personalities. Even the diabolical protagonist of the *Ecerinide*, the tyrant Ezzelino da Romano, has heroic and sympathetic facets to his character. So in Giotto, even in the cruelest scenes where the offenders' guilt is abundantly plain (like the *Kiss of Judas*, the *Massacre of the Innocents*, *Christ driving the Traders from the Temple*), even here the guilty, the villains, are not reduced to masks or caricatures but are shrewdly characterized with a thoroughly human touch; so that the conflict between good and evil develops and gains momentum on a broad plane of real antagonism. The *Kiss of Judas*, in which good and evil come face to face with such poignant intensity, would probably never have been possible without the rebirth of tragedy by then well under way in literature. The whole cycle of Giotto's frescos at Padua is, in a very real sense, founded on a dialogue, on an exchange of sharp and significant glances, while the Assisi frescos were rather in the nature of a sublime monologue, even in the scenes in which the moral and political heads of the Church, St Francis and the Pope, come together.

So it may well have been the circles in which he moved at Padua that prompted Giotto to humanize his figures and to adopt a realistic representation based on dialogue. But there is

LIFE OF CHRIST: THE KISS OF JUDAS, 1304-1305.
FRESCO, SCROVEGNI CHAPEL, PADUA.

a further element of novelty here: the physical characterization
of the figures, which indeed seems to be increasingly emphasized
as the work proceeds. We find human types of the most extraordinary realism: the shepherds in the *Nativity*, the sibyl in the

LIFE OF CHRIST: THE CRUCIFIXION, 1304-1305.
FRESCO, SCROVEGNI CHAPEL, PADUA.

Presentation in the Temple, the muleteer in the *Flight into Egypt*,
the fat man in the *Marriage at Cana*, Judas, the Moor in the
Scourging of Christ, the aged and exhausted Virgin of the *Ascension*
and the *Crucifixion*.

LIFE OF CHRIST: THE CRUCIFIXION, DETAIL: ANGELS, 1304-1305.
FRESCO, SCROVEGNI CHAPEL, PADUA.

This increasingly marked feature of his work, non-existent in Italian art before Giotto, must have developed under the influence of the University of Padua, where human character was an important object of study both in rhetoric and astrology, not for curiosity's sake but for the scientific interest attaching to it. Let it not be forgotten that after the Scrovegni Chapel frescos, from 1307, Giotto decorated the immense hall of the

Palazzo della Ragione in Padua with the largest set of paintings on astrological themes which had ever been seen, and which long remained the iconographic prototype of such works. We learn from documents that it gave a picture of the planets and astrological signs, based on a literary text drawn up by the famous physician and astrologer Pietro d'Abano, who returned

LIFE OF CHRIST: THE CRUCIFIXION, DETAIL: THE VIRGIN AND ST JOHN, 1304-1305. FRESCO, SCROVEGNI CHAPEL, PADUA.

to Padua from Paris in 1306; it was presumably intended to
represent a monumental horoscope of the city. This is not the
only instance of Giotto's interest in astrology; others have been
pointed out by Hartlaub. In the allegorical figures in monochrome in the Scrovegni Chapel he shows Prudence with the

F CHRIST AND NOLI ME TANGERE, 1304-1305.
CHAPEL, PADUA.

occult attribute of the mirror; and in the bas-reliefs of the
Campanile in Florence astrological themes recur three times.

Giotto's contacts with the cultural milieu of Padua thus
account for the novelty of his style and explain why he departed
from the more limited classicizing manner of the Assisi frescos.

LIFE OF JOACHIM: JOACHIM DRIVEN FROM THE TEMPLE, 1305-1306.
FRESCO, SCROVEGNI CHAPEL, PADUA.

But the powerful, rational, geometrically proportioned structure of the figures remains unchanged. Their full-bodied plasticity becomes even bolder, and a few foreshortenings also occur, while limpid colors underscore and bring out volumes. In short,

LIFE OF JOACHIM: THE ANNUNCIATION TO ST ANNE, 1305-1306.
FRESCO, SCROVEGNI CHAPEL, PADUA.

neither his naturalism (i.e. his direct approach to man) nor his
diminished sense of transcendence delivers Giotto from his
obsession with the law. Brought down from the heavens, God
triumphed on earth with equal power.

LIFE OF JOACHIM: THE MEETING AT THE GOLDEN GATE (DETAIL), 1305-1306.
FRESCO, SCROVEGNI CHAPEL, PADUA.

The episodes from the life of Joachim and the Virgin's childhood are a striking demonstration of Giotto's moral conception and realism. As compared with the over-compact narrative of the paintings beneath them, these scenes, added at the last minute, have too much space to develop in, and ample time for pauses and repetitions. Figures are few in number, with the result that the setting often rules supreme—the wilderness of *Joachim among the Shepherds*, and of the other

LIFE OF THE VIRGIN: THE BIRTH OF THE VIRGIN (DETAIL), 1305-1306.
FRESCO, SCROVEGNI CHAPEL, PADUA.

LIFE OF JOACHIM: JOACHIM'S SACRIFICE (DETAIL), 1305-1306.
FRESCO, SCROVEGNI CHAPEL, PADUA.

LIFE OF JOACHIM: JOACHIM'S DREAM (DETAIL), 1305-1306.
FRESCO, SCROVEGNI CHAPEL, PADUA.

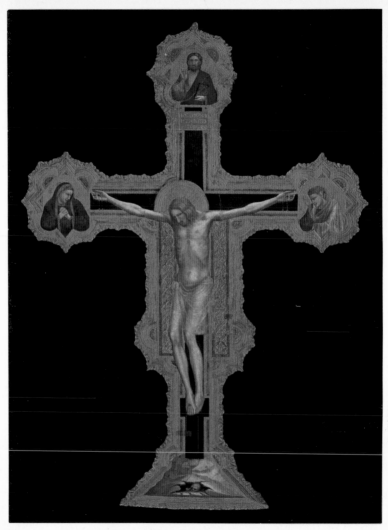

CRUCIFIX (WITH ASSISTANTS), 1306. ON WOOD.
MUSEO CIVICO, PADUA.

scenes of his hermit's life, and the homely domesticity of the *Annunciation to St Anne*. Here we find the direct antecedents of what later became known as the genre picture: shepherds with their flock, a maid-servant spinning, another laying out warm linen, plant life depicted with the painstaking accuracy of a botanist, musicians serenading a wedding procession. Yet few paintings are so intimately dramatic as these two sequences. Once again Giotto's genius for composing with a minimum of figures is given full scope and scales the heights. Sentimental and emotional expression finds its heroic sublimation in emptiness and silence. The same dramatic intensity and decision of style characterize the magnificent allegorical figures in monochrome along the base of the wall, which astonished his contemporaries, and which, in spite of their didactic tone, are perhaps the most convincing testimony of Giotto's literary and archeological culture. They testify, furthermore, to his ardent vocation as a sculptor, as a creator, that is, not so much of images as of idols.

Rather hasty and uninspired, on the other hand, in spite of the fully developed preliminary sketch on which they are based, are the paintings on the triumphal arch, with an *Annunciation* and related scenes indicative of the hurried conclusion to which the decoration was brought, in order no doubt to meet the deadline laid down for the consecration. An unqualified masterpiece, however, is the crucifix (now in the Museo Civico, Padua), which faithfully repeats the iconographical scheme of the Rimini crucifix, but with a new affective quality which gives it a matchless lyrical intensity. What Simone Martini succeeded in doing with his Madonnas, Giotto here achieved with the more intractable theme of the male nude, yet without sacrificing any of the cosmic, emblematic value of the Byzantine crucifixes. His modern interpretation is not a repudiation of the emotional values of medieval art, but a wonderful intensification of them.

THE VIRGIN AND CHILD WITH ANGELS, SHORTLY AFTER 1311. ON WOOD.
ALTAR PAINTING FROM THE CHURCH OF THE OGNISSANTI. UFFIZI, FLORENCE.

WORKS AFTER PADUA

THE documentary evidence relating to Giotto's activities after he left Padua is unfortunately very meager. The surviving paintings of this period differ markedly from one another; some present the stock repetitions of studio assistants. Inspired developments emerge, but it is impossible to tell in most cases whether their originality is due to Giotto himself or to his pupils, who by now had ripened into independent masters. Chronological points of reference are lacking, though the eventual identification of several coats of arms in the Bardi Chapel, probably alluding to a marriage, may be expected to provide a date or two. One cannot help being struck, however, by the fact that Giotto's activities in Florence seemed to increase in proportion as the power of the House of Anjou over Florence increased; and his departure for Naples, singularly enough, coincided with the death of Charles of Anjou and the advent of a new Florentine government. In any case the extant works in Florence extend roughly from 1311 to 1329 and cover only part of Giotto's final phase, of which we shall never know anything more owing to the total destruction of the great frescos in Naples and Milan.

However, in some altar paintings mainly by Giotto's hand and in the Santa Croce frescos we can trace a parallel evolution. The first works executed after his return to Florence show a certain archaism (due perhaps to the influence of Tuscan assistants) with respect to the frankly modern, Gothic character of the Scrovegni Chapel frescos. Thereafter he tended toward a greater refinement and elegance, especially in the idealization of feminine types, and toward a naturalistic treatment not only of settings and details but also of figures. This trend is made clear by a comparison of two very fine works, presumably separated by an interval of one or two decades: the Ognissanti

Madonna (Uffizi), executed, it is thought, shortly after his return to Florence, and the Madonna forming the central panel of a polyptych now divided between Washington, Chaalis and Florence, of unknown provenance, possibly executed during his stay in Naples, in any case a comparatively late work.

In the Uffizi Madonna Giotto reverts, and gives new life, to the old theme of the Virgin in Majesty, of the type with which he had already experimented in the Madonna of San Giorgio alla Costa. The monumentality of the Virgin, whose powerful anatomical structure shows through the heavy garments perhaps for the first time, has been extolled by all critics. Seen in perspective, the throne serves to focus our gaze on this supreme idol. Though not entirely justified by the elevation of the throne, the scale and volume of the figure are very imposing. This is not so much the Virgin as a goddess: unmoving and implacable, yet benevolent, like an allegory of Justice, to the iconographical type of which it closely approaches. Though a highly celebrated work, only a small part of it can safely be ascribed to Giotto himself: the Virgin's face and the two delightful figures of kneeling angels seen in profile. The angels and prophets above are by an archaizing pupil, perhaps Taddeo Gaddi, whose close collaboration with Giotto must have begun about this time; because of these archaizing figures the picture has usually been given too early a date.

His pupils, however, are not altogether to blame for the disequilibrium of the whole. An undeniable incongruity exists between the hieratic figure—with the carefully observed hierarchy of Virgin, angels and prophets—and the striking modernity of the severe, elongated face, with the curiously asymmetrical eyes and uncertain gaze, caught in a moment of hesitation and vague misgivings. This contrast appears even more marked when we turn to the face, rigid and rather banal, of the Christchild.

In the Washington Madonna, on the other hand, he again rises to the emotional plane, as in the Badia polyptych, but with the refinements now of a deeper, richer inner life—and this in spite of the fact that, as compared with the more humanized Madonnas of Duccio, Giotto sharply differentiates the Mother, solemn and self-absorbed, from the Child, deliberately gracile by contrast. The Virgin turns from playing with the Child, reaching for a flower, and gazes pensively into the future, or into our soul. In the saints on the dispersed side panels (Musée Jacquemart-André, Chaalis), with the exception of the inflexible, self-conscious figure of St Stephen (Museo Horne, Florence), there is an indefinable sense of expectancy and anguish. The muted color harmonies contribute to throw this romantic aura over the polyptych (which is also partly the work of studio assistants), while the Ognissanti Madonna is substantially grounded on a calculated discord of pure colors. It is as if the atmosphere mattered more than the event; the tone is no longer rational but emotional, not far removed from the spirituality of the Sienese. Design and color in this phase grow steadily softer and sweeter, culminating in an incomparable exquisiteness and grace, as exemplified in the infinite delicacy of the Bologna *Virgin and Child*, perhaps the only surviving testimony to more extensive activities in that city round about 1330. Not taste so much as temperament now distinguishes Giotto from Simone Martini. Significantly enough, it was a Madonna by Giotto in this style that Petrarch lovingly kept beside the "celestial" portrait of Laura by Simone Martini.

Even more surprising, and perhaps achieved within a very short time, is the parallel metamorphosis of style apparent in the two extant fresco cycles in Santa Croce, Florence: scenes of St John the Baptist and St John the Evangelist in the private chapel of the wealthy Peruzzi family, and scenes of St Francis in the adjacent chapel of the equally powerful Bardi family.

LIFE OF ST JOHN THE EVANGELIST: THE RAISING OF DRUSIANA (DETAIL),
AFTER 1311. FRESCO, PERUZZI CHAPEL, SANTA CROCE, FLORENCE.

LIFE OF ST JOHN THE EVANGELIST: THE RAISING OF DRUSIANA (DETAIL),
AFTER 1311. FRESCO, PERUZZI CHAPEL, SANTA CROCE, FLORENCE.

The latter frescos, anyhow the lower registers, must have been painted after 1317, date of the canonization of St Louis of Toulouse, who figures in them.

How much time elapsed between the two cycles, it is now impossible to say. Even after the admirable restoration recently carried out by Leonetto Tintori, they are seen to differ considerably as to their state of preservation. In the Peruzzi Chapel the composition has survived almost in its entirety, but the figures are reduced to little more than the ground painting, while in the Bardi Chapel, in spite of vast gaps in the composition, the uppermost layer of paint has been preserved, even to the most minute finishing touches. This circumstance only serves to emphasize the substantial and decidedly mysterious divergence between them, which cannot be due alone to the presence of different collaborators or to the fact that in the scenes of the two Ss John Giotto was faced with an entirely new theme, while in the life of St Francis he had a subject long familiar to him; in reality, the most novel aspects of the work are to be found precisely in the scenes with St Francis. It would seem, rather, that in the Peruzzi Chapel the monumental handling of the stories of the two Ss John—patron saints of Florence—sprang from the need to invest them with an official character.

These frescos, which with those in the Bardi Chapel remained the basis of the enthusiastic appreciation of Giotto shown by the Renaissance masters, are in many ways a recasting of Paduan themes. He reverted here to solutions already worked out in the stories of Joachim and the childhood of the Virgin, but applied them now with a more rhythmical expressiveness and a certain affectation of style which, by no mere chance, deliberately rhetorical devices that they were, appealed to the 16th-century Mannerists. The characterization of figures, though carried very far, is nevertheless stifled by the concern for too

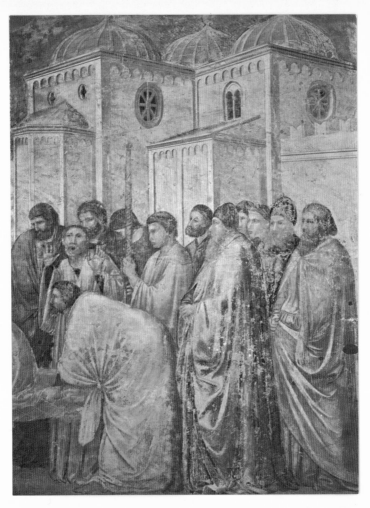

LIFE OF ST JOHN THE BAPTIST: THE BIRTH OF ST JOHN (DETAIL),
AFTER 1311. FRESCO, PERUZZI CHAPEL, SANTA CROCE, FLORENCE.

LIFE OF ST FRANCIS: THE SAINT RENOUNCING THE WORLD (DETAIL),
AFTER 1311. FRESCO, BARDI CHAPEL, SANTA CROCE, FLORENCE.

rigid and static a monumentality, to some degree made necessary by the large dimensions of the scenes. The background, an incongruous mixture of Roman-Cosmatesque and Paduan-Romanesque elements, fulfils a function that is coloristic more than anything else. Everywhere the colors are calculated and severe, with accents here and there of great intensity, and with symmetrical reiterations from scene to scene; the customary linear design defining facial contours and giving expression to glances has vanished with the deterioration of the frescos. What we find instead is an admirably precise, symmetrical, faultless facial structure, which coincides in several groups with a power of synthesis and association that brings to mind Masaccio and Michelangelo. Leading figures again rise to heroic heights, as at Assisi, though the passionate enthusiasm of youth has now waned; even the bystanders witnessing the saint's miracles seem to assume the serenity and formal dignity of Titans. It is curious to note that attitudes and gestures, almost as if to take the place of a colloquy between the leading figures, acquire a didactic function; they seem to engage us in the action, and make so direct an appeal to us that they compel us, as it were, to share the moods and states of mind of the heroes portrayed. Giotto succeeds in lending his painting all the expressive power of direct speech, of history in the making.

In the Bardi Chapel, on the other hand—except in the lunettes, which are of inferior quality and even more Paduan in style than the same frescos in the Peruzzi Chapel—the prevailing tone is lyrical and legendary, in a coloristic atmosphere of subtle refinement which suggests the helping hand of some Sienese collaborator. Here, where the state of preservation is much better, we can also distinguish the work of different assistants and note one or two expedients (the use of identical profiles, for example, varied only by means of different head-dresses or adjuncts) resorted to in order to accelerate

Gi. 51

LIFE OF THE FRANCIS: THE ORDEAL BY FIRE, DETAIL: A MOORISH PRIEST,
AFTER 1317. FRESCO, BARDI CHAPEL, SANTA CROCE, FLORENCE.

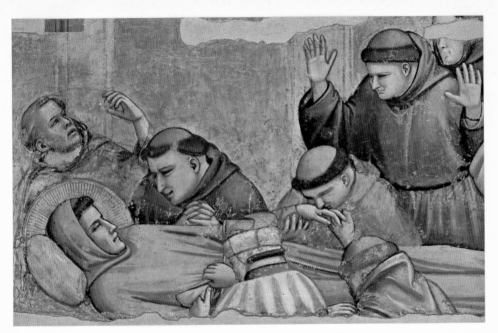

LIFE OF ST FRANCIS: THE SAINT'S DEATH (DETAIL), AFTER 1317.
FRESCO, BARDI CHAPEL, SANTA CROCE, FLORENCE.

anger, and the agitated crowd surges around him. In the
Ordeal by Fire, taking place before the Sultan, the Moorish
priests are handled with an admirable freedom of movement
and the classic tetramorph turns into a Gothic round. The
solemn, epic exaltation of Assisi has altogether vanished.
The saint's miraculous apparition in the chapter-house at Arles
occurs in an atmosphere of unruffled serenity and composure,
while his death and subsequent apparitions take place quietly
and intimately, seeming to fall naturally into the round of daily
events. A warm sense of humanity and a deeper comprehension

of the inner life amply compensate for the absence of heroics. With the passing of the years, and the approach of old age, Giotto turned his eyes increasingly inward.

Here, in the Bardi Chapel, one looks eagerly for direct traces of his hand, for tokens of his living presence, as he worked intently day by day on the scaffolding. But at this point arises the knottiest problem of all. Beside the body of St Francis appears the figure of a friar, which looks as if it had been inserted at the last minute to balance a composition too heavily weighted on the right. When Taddeo Gaddi came to paint the same scene, he suppressed the figure. A glance at this friar is enough for us to note his age and physique and divine his psychological processes; he is not a type figure but an individual such as might still be met today in the cloisters of Santa Croce. The same mimetic capacity appears in the extraordinary figure facing us, in the group of Moorish priests, with his angry glance and half-open mouth, and appears to some extent too in his companions and the Sultan. And again, most strikingly, in the monk shown drawing aside the curtain in the *Visions of Fra Agostino and of the Bishop of Assisi*. Whose was the hand that added, apparently at the last moment, these masterly touches, arresting in their modernity, which fit so perfectly into the whole? Was it his pupil Stefano, the "ape of nature," as he was called, or Giotto himself, to whom nature seemed to have granted every gift unstintingly?

There is no answering that question without some knowledge of the other fundamental aspect of Giotto's genius, now hidden forever in the mists of time. I refer to his profane works, such as the allegorical frescos of the "Comune Rubato" in the Palazzo del Podestà, Florence (which presumably served as a model for Ambrogio Lorenzetti's celebrated frescos in the Palazzo Pubblico, Siena), the cycle of famous men at Naples, or the "Vana Gloria" surrounded by ancient and modern heroes in Milan. Here was the worldly-minded Giotto, unconcerned with religious and devotional questions, freely demonstrating perhaps, as no one else could, how truly universal painting was, how superlatively "natural" and "noble" an art it could be without infringing the rules of "measure" and perspective.

Here we might have seen the master capable of introducing and even creating the profane iconography needed to give solemn and splendid expression to civic glories. It may be that the heirs of this great cultural legacy are to be sought for in Siena rather than Florence, and rather in Northern Gothic art than in Italy. Certainly, with the loss of these masterpieces we are deprived not only of the crowning works of Giotto's career, but also perhaps of a new way of seeing the world. They might have provided the key that would have enabled us to understand how, in the political and cultural ferment of the most enlightened courts of the day, where Giotto was welcomed as the first "court painter" in the modern sense, the transition was accomplished from the exclusively sacred painting of the Middle Ages to profane painting. That Giotto in his old age resolutely devoted himself to the latter seems to be borne out by the only remaining testimony of this final phase: the decorative system which he designed for the Campanile in Florence; here the exquisite, distinctly Gothic polychromy of the marbles and the supple freedom of the structures, now in no wise classicizing, are combined with the most moving representation of the arts and sciences that European humanism ever produced.

★

Giotto died in 1337 just as Pope Benedict XII was about to summon him to Avignon. There he would probably have met Simone Martini—perhaps not for the first time—and his style might then have spread beyond Italy to the whole of Europe. By way of the Renaissance masters, however, who venerated him as their greatest ancestor, his style finally brought its influence to bear on the whole of Western art. Or rather, more than his style, the great problem he set himself to solve in his paintings: that of reconciling mind and matter, sacred and profane, idea and action, geometrical structure (following the principles of Vitruvius) and nature.

The whole of the Renaissance can by no means be said to lie in this achievement. And indeed a case might easily be made out for seeing in Giotto, more than anything else, one of the summits of classicism. But whether we link him up with the Renaissance or with classicism, it must be acknowledged that he worked out pictorial solutions which for centuries set the standard of Western art, whose visual categories he virtually created. What his career shows us is that Giotto understood, as few others have, that there is no abstract law, but that the idea, if it is to dominate the course of human history, must sustain and foster man's aspirations, and to do so must be adapted to time and place. He and his restless, eventful career might well be symbolized by the emblem of Leonardo: the mariner's compass whose needle holds fast to the pole, even though the currents of the sea and the will of the navigator are continually changing the latitude and even the hemisphere of the ship's course; for a fixed purpose, coherently pursued, does not necessarily mean a fixed course.

SELECTED BIBLIOGRAPHY

INDEX OF NAMES AND PLACES

CONTENTS

SELECTED BIBLIOGRAPHY

The following bibliography lists the monographs, essays and articles referred to, explicitly or implicitly, in the text. Comprehensive bibliographies are to be found in such works as R. SALVINI, *Bibliografia Giottesca*, Rome 1938, which contains a virtually complete list of all publications on Giotto up to 1937, and R. OERTEL, *Wende der Giotto-Forschung*, in *Zeitschrift für Kunstgeschichte*, 1943-1944, 1-2, pp. 1-27. As regards the paintings, consult the monumental catalogue of the Mostra Giottesca held in Florence in 1937: G. SINIBALDI and G. BRUNETTI, *Pittura Italiana del Duecento e Trecento*, Florence 1943, in which the various arguments concerning the chronology, authenticity and authorship of the works are set forth. The most recent and comprehensive monographs on Giotto are those of R. SALVINI, Milan 1952, and C. GNUDI, Milan 1958 (Italian and French editions); the latter contains (pp. 251-253) an extensive bibliography covering the years 1937-1958.

The standard work on the social and cultural milieu in which Giotto lived and worked is that of F. ANTAL, *Florentine Painting and its Social Background*, London 1948, which also deals very acutely with Giotto himself.

I am indebted to the following works and articles for the assistance they have given me in writing this book:

General Works

L. VENTURI, *Introduzione all'arte di Giotto*, in *L'Arte*, XXII, 1919, pp. 49-56. — Erwin ROSENTHAL, *Giotto*, Augsburg 1924. — L. VENTURI, *Gusto dei Primitivi*, Bologna 1926. — J. SCHLOSSER, *Präludien, Vorträge und Aufsätze*, Berlin 1927 (*Zur Geschichte der Kunstbiographie*, pp. 248 ff.). — G. L. LUZZATTO, *L'arte di Giotto*, Bologna 1928. — M. SALMI, *Musaici e pittura del secolo XIII a Firenze*, in *Dedalo*, 1931. — E. CECCHI, *Giotto*, Milan 1937. — V. MARIANI, *Giotto*, Rome 1937. — L. COLETTI, *Esordi di Giotto*, in *La Critica d'Arte*, June 1937, pp. 104-107. — R. MAZZUCCONI, *Giotto*, Florence 1938. — C. BRANDI, *Giotto*, in *Le Arti*, 1938-1939, pp. 5-21, 116-131. — T. HETZER, *Giotto*, Frankfort 1941. — L. COLETTI, *I Primitivi*, I, Novara 1941. — P. TOESCA, *Giotto*, Turin 1941. — M. RABINOVSZKY, *L'umanità di Giotto*, in *Janus Pannonius* I, 1947, No. 2-3, pp. 320-336. — L. VENTURI, *Italian Painting*, vol. I: *The Creators of the Renaissance*, Geneva 1950. — P. TOESCA, *Il Trecento*, Turin 1951. — C. BRANDI, *Duccio*, Florence 1951. — P. D'ANCONA, *Giotto*, Milan 1953. — C. L. RAGGHIANTI, *Pittura del Dugento a Firenze*, Sele Arte Monografie, Florence 1955. — E. CARLI, *La Renaissance du Réalisme au Moyen Age italien*, in *L'Art et l'Homme*, II, Paris 1958, pp. 343-352. — C. GNUDI, *Giotto*, in *I Maestri della Pittura Italiana*, Epoca, Milan 1959.

Giotto and his Times

M. Dvořák, *Idealismus und Naturalismus in der gotischen Skulptur und Malerei*, Munich-Berlin 1918. — E. Rosenthal, *Giotto in der mittelalterlichen Geistesentwicklung*, Augsburg 1924. — G. Fiocco, *Giotto e Arnolfo*, in *Rivista d'Arte*, 1937, No. 3-4, pp. 221-239. — M. Salmi, *Le origini di Giotto*, in *Rivista d'Arte*, 1937, No. 3-4, pp. 193-220. — G. Weise, *Die geistige Welt der Gotik und ihre Bedeutung für Italien*, Halle 1939. — H. Jantzen, *Giotto und der gotische Stil*, Das *Werk des Künstlers*, I, 1939-1940. — W. Paatz, *Italien und die künstlerischen Bewegungen der Gotik in der Renaissance*, in *Römisches Jahrbuch für Kunstgeschichte*, V, 1941, pp. 163-222. — D. Frey, *Giotto und die maniera greca*, in *Wallraf Richartz Jahrbuch*, Cologne, 14, 1952, pp. 73 ff. — A. Bush-Brown, *Giotto. Two Problems in the Origin of his Style*, in *Art Bulletin*, March 1952. — Kurt Bauch, *Die geschichtliche Bedeutung von Giottos Frühstil*, in *Mitteilungen des kunsthistorischen Instituts in Florenz*, 1953, VII, pp. 43-64. — G. Weise, *L'Italia e il Mondo gotico*, Florence 1956.

On Perspective:

G. J. Kern, *Die Anfänge der zentralperspektivischen Konstruktion in der italienischen Malerei des 14. Jahrhunderts*, in *Mitteilungen des kunsthistorischen Instituts in Florenz*, 1912-1917, pp. 39-65.

Giotto's Relations with the Franciscan Order:

H. Schrade, *Franz von Assisi und Giotto*, in *Archiv für Kunstgeschichte*, XVII, 1927, pp. 150 ff. — H. B. Gutman, *The Rebirth of the Fine Arts and Franciscan Thought*, in *Franciscan Studies*, September 1945, pp. 215-234, March 1946, pp. 1 ff. — G. Francastel, *Du Byzantin à la Renaissance*, in *Histoire de la Peinture Italienne*, vol. I, Paris 1955; English translation, *From the Byzantine Masters to the Renaissance*, New York 1959. — P. Francastel, *L'Art italien et le rôle personnel de saint François*, in *Annales*, XI, October-December 1956, No. 4, pp. 482-489.

Giotto and Dante:

P. L. Rambaldi, *Dante e Giotto nella letteratura artistica sino al Vasari*, in *Rivista d'Arte*, 1937, No. 3-4, pp. 286-348. — F. Rossi, *La data della cappella del Podestà*, in *Giotto e il suo Mugello*, Florence 1937.

Giotto's Relations with Sienese Art (limited to articles dealing exclusively with this subject):

G. Sinibaldi, *Come Lorenzo Ghiberti sentisse Giotto ed Ambrogio Lorenzetti*, in *L'Arte*, XXXI, 1928, pp. 80-82. — Andrew Peter, *Giotto and Ambrogio Lorenzetti*, in *Burlington Magazine*, 1940, I, pp. 3-8. — C. Gnudi, *Grandezza di Simone*, in *Scritti di Storia dell'Arte in onore di Lionello Venturi*, Rome 1956, I, pp. 87-100.

The Works

Giotto's Early Florentine Works:

U. PROCACCI, *La patria di Giotto*, in *Giotto e il suo Mugello*, Florence 1937, pp. 9-16.

The Santa Maria Novella Crucifix:

R. LONGHI, *Giudizio sul Duecento*, in *Proporzioni* II, 1948, pp. 5 ff. — S. ORLANDI, O. P., *S. Maria Novella e i suoi chiostri monumentali*, Florence 1956. — W. SCHÖNE, *Giottos Kruzifixustafeln und ihre Vorgänger*, in *Festschrift Friedrich Winkler*, Berlin 1959, pp. 49-63.

The Madonna of San Giorgio alla Costa:

See the reconstitution in R. OFFNER, *A Critical and Historial Corpus of Florentine Painting*, III, 6, New York 1956.

The Assisi Frescos:

P. JOHANSEN, *Giotto in Assisi*, in *Jahrbuch für Kunstwissenschaft*, 1930, p. 130. — Frank Jewett MATHER Jr., *The Isaac Master*, Princeton 1932. — Frank Jewett MATHER Jr., *Giotto's St. Francis Series at Assisi historically considered*, in *Art Bulletin*, June 1943, pp. 97-111. — P. TOESCA, *Assisi, Gli Affreschi della vita di S. Francesco*, Artis Monumenta Photographice Edita, Florence 1946 et seq. — P. MURRAY, *Notes on Some Early Giotto Sources*, in *Journal of the Warburg and Courtauld Institutes*, 1953, XVI, pp. 58-86. — F. D. KLINGENDER, *St. Francis and the Birds of the Apocalypse*, in *Journal of the Warburg and Courtauld Institutes*, XVI, 1953, pp. 13-23. — M. Roy FISHER, *Assisi, Padua and the Boy in the Tree*, in *Art Bulletin*, 1956, pp. 47 ff. — P. TOESCA, *Una postilla alla "Vita di San Francesco" nella chiesa superiore di Assisi*, in *Studies in the History of Art dedicated to William E. Suida*, London 1959. — Millard MEISS will shortly publish the tabulation of work-days spent on the Assisi frescos, based on Leonetto TINTORI's examination of them. — On the iconography of the Assisi frescos, consult H. SCHRADE, *Bibliche Figurazioni*, in *Enciclopedia Universale dell'Arte*, II, col. 566-567.

St Peter's, Rome:

F. M. TORRIGGIO, *Le Sacre Grotte Vaticane*, Viterbo 1618, passim. — E. MÜNTZ, in *Mélanges d'Archéologie et d'Histoire de l'Ecole française de Rome*, 1881, I, pp. 111-137. — E. MÜNTZ and FROTHINGHAM, *Il tesoro della Basilica di San Pietro in Vaticano dal XIII al XV secolo*, in *Archivio della R. Società Romana di Storia Patria*, VI, 1883, pp. 81-92. — P. EGIDI, *Necrologi e libri affini della provincia di Roma*, Rome 1908. — L. VENTURI, *La data dell'attività romana di Giotto*, in *L'Arte*, 1918, p. 229. — P. FEDELI, *La data dell'attività romana di Giotto*, in *Archivio della R. Società Romana di Storia Patria*, Rome 1918, pp. 353-361. — W. KÖRTE, *Die "Navicella" des Giotto*, in *Festschrift Wilhelm Pinder*, Leipzig 1938, pp. 223-263. — W. PAESELER, *Giottos Navicella und ihr spätantikes Vorbild*, in *Römisches Jahrbuch für*

Kunstgeschichte, V, 1941, pp. 49-162. — W. Fritz VOLLBACH, *Tabula cum imaginibus apostolorum Petri et Pauli*, in *Orientalia Christiana Periodica*, XIII, 1947, pp. 369-375. — A. FRUGONI, *La figura e l'opera del cardinale Jacopo Stefaneschi*, in *Rendiconti dell'Accademia Nazionale dei Lincei*, VIII, vol. 7-10, 1950. — M. GOSEBRUCH, *Giottos römischer Stefaneschi-Altar und die Fresken des sog. "Maestro delle Vele" in der Unterkirche S. Francesco zu Assisi*, in *Kunstchronik*, XI, October 1958, pp. 288-291. — E. BATTISTI, *Simbolo e classicismo*, in *Rinascimento e Barocco*, Turin 1960.

St John Lateran, Rome :

The frescos as a whole are described by PANVINIUS, in *De Praecipuis Urbis Romae basilicis*, Rome 1570, pp. 231-232. — C. MITCHELL, *The Lateran Fresco of Boniface VIII*, in *Journal of the Warburg and Courtauld Institutes*, XIV, 1951, No. 1-2, pp. 1-6. — *Roma Nobilis*, edited by Igino Cecchetti, Rome 1952. — C. BRANDI, *Giotto recuperato a San Giovanni Laterano*, in *Scritti di Storia dell'Arte in onore di Lionello Venturi*, Rome 1956, I, pp. 55-85.

Polyptych from the Badia (Florence, Uffizi) :

This work was identified by U. PROCACCI, in *Miscellanea di Storia dell'Arte in onore di Mario Salmi*, Rome 1960. — Fragments of frescos discovered by U. PROCACCI in the Badia of Florence will be published very shortly.

Rimini :

G. SINIBALDI, *Il Crocifisso del Tempio Malatestiano di Rimini*, in *Zeitschrift für Kunstgeschichte*, X, 1941-1942, pp. 289 ff. — F. ZERI, *Due appunti su Giotto*, in *Paragone*, 85, January 1957, pp. 75-87.

Scrovegni Chapel, Padua :

Domenico Maria FEDERICI, *Istoria de' Cavalieri Gaudenti*, Treviso 1787. — W. ARSLAN, *A conferma di una ipotesi dimenticata*, in *Il Popolo Veneto*, June 6, 1923. — E. F. ROTHSCHILD and E. H. WILKINS, *Hell in the Florentine Baptistery Mosaic and in Giotto's Paduan Fresco*, in *Art Studies*, 1928, pp. 31-35. — A. MOSCHETTI, *Padova al tempo di Giotto*, in *Bollettino del Museo Civico di Padova*, 1933, pp. 63-86. — C. RONCHI, *Un documento inedito del 9 gennaio 1305 intorno alla Cappella degli Scrovegni*, in *Atti e Memorie dell'Accademia di Scienze, Lettere ed Arti di Padova*, LII, 1935-1936, III, pp. 210 ff. — F. BAUMGART, *Die Fresken Giottos in der Arena Kapelle zu Padua*, in *Zeitschrift für Kunstgeschichte*, 1937, pp. 1-31. — M. L. BONIFAZI, *Giotto e le figurazioni allegoriche delle virtù e dei vizi*, in *Illustrazione Vaticana*, Rome 1937, No. 14, July, pp. 16-31. — H. JANTZEN, *Die zeitliche Abfolge der Paduaner Fresken Giottos*, in *Jahrbuch der Preuss. Kunstsammlungen*, LX, 1939, pp. 187 ff. — M. ALPATOFF, *The Parallelism of Giotto's Paduan Frescoes*, in *Art Bulletin*, September 1947, pp. 149-154. — A. PROSDOCIMI, *Sul Crocifisso di Giotto della Cappella degli Scrovegni ; primitiva collocazione e restauri*, in *Bollettino del Museo Civico di Padova*, 1956, pp. 65-82. — Dorothy C. SHORR, *The Role of the Virgin in Giotto's Last Judgment*, in *Art Bulletin*, December 1956, pp. 207-214. — U. SCHLEGEL, *Zum Bildprogramm der Arena-Kapelle*, in *Zeitschrift für Kunstgeschichte*, XX, 1957, 1, pp. 125-146. — C. GNUDI, *Il passo di Riccobaldo Ferrarese relativo a Giotto e il problema della sua autenticità*, in *Studies in the History of Art dedicated to William E. Suida*, London 1959, pp. 26-30. — Millard MEISS will shortly publish the tabulation of work-days spent on the frescos in the Scrovegni Chapel, based on Leonetto TINTORI's examination of them in the course of restoration.

Astrological Cycle in the Palazzo della Ragione, Padua:

A. MOSCHETTI, *Principale palatium*, in *Bollettino del Museo Civico di Padova*, new series, VIII, 1932, IX, 1933 and X-XI, 1934-1939. — G. H. HARTLAUB, *Giottos zweites Hauptwerk in Padua*, in *Zeitschrift für Kunstwissenschaft*, IV, 1950, pp. 19-34.

Santa Croce, Florence:

L. CHIAPPELLI, *Nuovi documenti su Giotto*, in *L'Arte*, vol. XXVI, 1923, pp. 132-136. — Jule GY-WILDE, *Giotto-Studien*, in *Wiener Jahrbuch für Kunstgeschichte* VII, 1930, pp. 45-94. — R. G. MATHER, *Nuove informazioni relative alle matricole di Giotto, ecc.; nell'arte dei medici e speziali*, in *L'Arte*, January 1936, pp. 50-64. — G. MARCHINI, *Gli affreschi perduti di Giotto in una cappella di S. Croce*, in *Rivista d'Arte* XX, 1938, pp. 815 ff. (with a reconstitution of the frescos in the Tosinghi and Spinelli Chapels, based on replicas and imitations of the 14th century. The *Dormition of the Virgin* in Berlin Museum seems to link up with the decorations in these chapels. — U. PROCACCI will shortly publish a report of the restorations carried out in the Bardi and Peruzzi Chapels, together with a tabulation of the work-days based on the observations of Leonetto Tintori.

Allegorical Frescos, Florence:

S. MORPURGO, *Brutus, il buon giudice, nell'Udienza dell'Arte della Lana*, in *Miscellanea di Storia dell'Arte in onore di I. B. Supino*, Florence 1933, pp. 159 ff.

Polyptych divided between Washington, Chaalis and Museo Horne, Florence:

R. LONGHI, *Progresso nella reintegrazione di un polittico di Giotto*, in *Dedalo*, XI, p. 285.

Bologna:

L. FRATI, *Giotto a Bologna*, in *L'Arte*, 1910, pp. 466.

Naples:

G. DE BLASIIS, *Immagini di uomini famosi in una sala di Castelnuovo attribuiti a Giotto*, in *Napoli Nobilissima*, IV, 1900, p. 65. — See also M. SALMI,

Contributi fiorentini alla Storia dell'Arte, in *Atti e Memorie dell'Accademia fiorentina "La Colombaria"*, 1943-1946, pp. 415-420, attributing to Maso di Banco the few fragments found in the Castelnuovo at Naples.

The Campanile in Florence :

See the drawing (Museo dell'Opera del Duomo, Siena) which appears to represent the initial project. Cf. P. TOESCA, *Il Trecento*, Turin 1951, pp. 18-20, and note 12. — R. SALVINI, *Giotto architetto*, in *Illustrazione Toscana*, April 1937, pp. 33-35. — W. BRAUNFELS, *Giottos Campanile*, in *Das Münster*, I, 1947-1948, pp. 193 ff.

Milan :

G. GIULINI, *Memorie spettanti alla storia, al governo ed alla descrizione della città e campagna di Milano ne' secoli bassi*, Milan 1771, pp. 330 ff. — A. MARABOTTINI, *Giovanni da Milano*, Florence 1950. —M. SALMI, *La pittura e la miniatura gotica in Lombardia*, in *Storia di Milano*, 1955, vol. V., pp. 815 ff.

On Giotto's being invited to go to Avignon :

B. PLATINA, *Liber de vita Christi ac Pontificum omnium*, Venice 1479, c. 172. — M. E. CASTELNUOVO, *Questioni Italo-Avignonesi*, in *CIXᵉ Congrès International d'Histoire de l'Art*, Paris, September 1958.

We take pleasure here in expressing our grateful thanks for advice and assistance received from Messrs E. ARSLAN, C. GNUDI, L. GROSSATO, A. MARABOTTINI, U. MIDDELDORF, M. MURARO, U. PROCACCI, P. ROSSI, M. SALMI, F. SANTI, L. TINTORI, A. VALLONE, L. VENTURI.

INDEX OF NAMES AND PLACES

CONTENTS

THIS VOLUME, THE THIRTY-SECOND OF THE COLLECTION "THE TASTE OF OUR TIME", WAS PRODUCED BY THE TECHNICAL STAFF OF EDITIONS D'ART ALBERT SKIRA, FINISHED THE FIFTEENTH DAY OF MARCH NINETEEN HUNDRED AND SIXTY

TEXT AND ILLUSTRATIONS BY THE

SKIRA

COLOR STUDIO
AT IMPRIMERIES RÉUNIES S.A., LAUSANNE

PLATES ENGRAVED BY GUEZELLE ET RENOUARD, PARIS

COLOR PHOTOGRAPHS BY CLAUDIO EMMER, MILAN

PRINTED IN SWITZERLAND